The Vilna Vegetarian Cookbook

אוגערקעס
Cucumbers

קעלרעפע
Cole-rape

קאלפיער
Cauli flower

שפינאק
Spinage

פאמידארן
Toma toes

גרינע ארבעסלעך
Green peas

מערן
Carrot

פרעש
Leek

קרויט
Cabbage

The Vilna Vegetarian Cookbook

FANIA LEWANDO

Translated from the Yiddish, annotated, and adapted
for the modern kitchen by Eve Jochnowitz

Foreword by Joan Nathan

SCHOCKEN BOOKS, NEW YORK

Published in the United States by Schocken Books,
a division of Random House LLC, New York, and distributed
in Canada by Random House of Canada Limited, Toronto,
Penguin Random House companies. Originally published in Vilna
in Yiddish as *Vegetarish-Dietisher Kokhbukh* by G. Kleckina in 1938.

Schocken Books and colophon are registered trademarks of Random House LLC.

Library of Congress Cataloging-in-Publication Data
Lewando, Fania, author.
[Vegetarish-Dietisher Kokhbukh. English]
The Vilna Vegetarian Cookbook / Fania Lewando ; translated from the Yiddish,
annotated, and adapted for the modern kitchen by Eve Jochnowitz ; foreword
by Joan Nathan.
pages cm
Includes index.
ISBN 978-0-8052-4327-7 (hardcover : alk. paper). ISBN 978-0-8052-4328-4 (eBook).
1. Jewish cooking.   2. Vegetarian cooking.   3. Cooking (natural foods)
I. Jochnowitz, Eve, translator.   II. Title.
TX724.L45 2015   641.5'636—dc23   2014031579

www.schocken.com

Book design by Soonyoung Kwon
Cover design by Kelly Blair

Printed in China
First Edition
2 4 6 8 9 7 5 3 1

Dedicated to the memory of Fania Lewando,
a pioneering thinker and cook
and a passionate educator, who devoted her life
to promoting health and vitality

איטאַליעגישע קרויט (װאָלאָסקע)
Italien Cabbage

רעטעכלעך
Radishes

ציבעלע
Onion

בוריקעס
Beet-roots

Contents

Salads

Soups

Cutlets

Stewed Dishes

Miscellaneous Dishes

Blintzes (Stuffed Crepes)

Omelets

Porridges

Frittatas

Kugels with Cholents

Puddings

Latkes

Passover Foods

Substantial Puddings

Sauces and Creams

Stuffed Foods

Baked Goods

Jams and Preserves

Turnovers

Compotes and Desserts

Glazes and Garnishes for Cakes

Coffee, Buttermilk, and Yogurt

Marinated Foods

Ices

Wine, Mead, and Liqueur

Vitamin Drinks and Juices

קרוטשקע (בוּרקעס)
Turnip

רויטע קרויט
Red Cabbage

Foreword

JOAN NATHAN

A few years ago, when I was giving a lecture before Passover at the Stone Barns Center for Food and Agriculture in Pocantico Hills, in Westchester County, New York, two women with a mission, Barbara Mazur and Wendy Waxman, came to hear me speak.

They also brought a manuscript.

When I saw this English translation of Fania Lewando's vegetarian cookbook, originally published in Vilna in Yiddish in 1938 as *Vegetarish-Dietisher Kokhbukh: 400 Shpeizn Gemakht Oysshlislekh fun Grinsn (Vegetarian-Dietetic Cookbook: 400 Recipes Made Exclusively from Vegetables)*, I was struck by the beauty of its colorful illustrations and the wide range of its vegetarian recipes. I immediately contacted Altie Karper, editorial director of Schocken Books, and told her about the importance of this splendid book.

Because of the very nature of the laws of *kashrut*—which include the separation of meat and dairy dishes—Jewish cuisine has always included many vegetarian recipes. Also, many Jews have felt that being a vegetarian was a step toward increased spirituality, because by refraining from eating fish and meat they were avoiding the necessity of slaughtering living beings. In early-twentieth-century Palestine, when there was little meat available to the immigrant Jews, vegetable dishes became increasingly popular. Meanwhile, in Europe, as Hitler's menace loomed on the horizon, anti-Semitic measures that prohibited the traditional Jewish ritual slaughtering of animals and poultry were enacted into law, starting in Polish-occupied Vilna in 1935. In response, Yiddish and German kosher cookbooks offered recipes for meatless meals, recipes that eventually made their way to Palestine.

But until that moment in Westchester County, I knew nothing about Fania Lewando or her cookbook. Barbara and Wendy, while visiting the offices of the YIVO Institute for Jewish Research in New York, happened upon this jewel—one of a very few extant copies. As soon as I saw it, I realized that they had discovered a piece of Jewish culinary history that must be told and shared. Appetizing illustrations of kohlrabi, tomatoes, peppers, and a dozen other fruits and vegetables are sprinkled throughout its pages, color drawings adapted from bilingual seed packets sold in Europe and in Palestine.

Jewish women have a significant history of publishing cookbooks. Rebekka Wolf's *Kokhbukh für Israelitische Frauen* (*Cookbook for Jewish Women*) was first published in Berlin in the early 1850s and stayed in print for decades, and in 1871 Esther Jacobs Levy published the *Jewish Cookery Book,* the first kosher cookbook to appear in America. (Levy went to the Library of Congress to register the book herself.) Dr. Erna Meyer wrote *How to Cook in Palestine* in German, English, and Hebrew, and with scarcely a meat recipe; it was published in Tel Aviv in 1936 by the H.N.Z., Palestine Federation of WIZO (Women's International Zionist Organization). But Fania Lewando was the first woman to publish a Yiddish-language vegetarian cookbook in Europe.

A pioneer in the emerging Jewish vegetarian movement, Lewando was the owner of a kosher dairy restaurant on the border of the Jewish quarter in old Vilnius (it's now a lawyer's office), and ran a kosher cooking school nearby. The restaurant was also a salon for Vilna's artists and writers. Her guest book includes comments and autographs from many luminaries, including the artist Marc Chagall and the Yiddish poet and playwright Itzik Manger. Lewando also supervised a kosher vegetarian kitchen on the ocean liner MS *Batory,* which traveled between Gdynia (near Gdańsk), Poland, and New York from 1936 to 1939.

Lewando, who was born in 1887, broke from the long-standing Eastern European custom of associating meat-based meals with the Sabbath, holidays, weddings, and other celebratory events, and vegetarian dishes with times of scarcity, with mourning, and with ordinary weekday meals. With words that still ring true today, Lewando created a Jewish culinary palette that celebrated nature's bounty. In meatless meals, long viewed as indicators of hardship and sorrow, Lewando found bright flavor and the key to health and well-being. She updated traditional recipes and introduced new ones, which can be updated again today by home chefs looking for healthier alternatives to ingredients such as butter, eggs, sugar, and sour cream. For example, I made the summer-squash-and-celeriac soup but replaced the cream sauce with yogurt. It was delicious.

Tragically, like too many other European Jews, this woman who devoted her life to promoting longevity perished sometime in 1941 or shortly thereafter, as she and her husband, an egg dealer named Lazar Lewando, were trying to flee the ghetto in which Vilna's Jews had been confined by the Nazis.

But, thanks to the perseverance of Barbara Mazur and Wendy Waxman, the translation and the recipe testing of Eve Jochnowitz, and the good shepherding of Altie Karper and Lexy Bloom at Schocken Books, the English-speaking world will now be graced with these timeless recipes.

קֶאפּעֶרעֶק
Fennel

טעֶרקישעֶר פּעֶפּעֶר
Red pepper

Translator's Preface

EVE JOCHNOWITZ

Translating and adapting Fania Lewando's vegetarian cookbook proved a rich experience with some unexpected challenges. The project involved falling into conversation with this remarkable and entirely original writer and cook. Lewando's prescriptive voice instructed me sternly at every step and guided me gently at every difficulty. Her fierce devotion to Jewish vegetarianism and her particular idiolects in language and in kitchen techniques are the pillars of this text.

CULINARY LEXICOGRAPHY

Lewando's vocabulary combines elements from diverse Yiddish regions, but her grammar places her solidly in her adopted city of Vilna. The first words of the book, *"tsu di baleboste"* ("to the housewife"), are expressed in northeastern Yiddish (standard Yiddish is *"tsu der baleboste"*).

Yiddish botanical terms vary from region to region and are occasionally misleading. *"Shvartse yagdes"* is one of the common Yiddish words for "blueberries" *(Vaccinium),* but a casual reader might understandably take it to mean "blackberries." Lewando uses two words for "Jerusalem artichokes" (translation of "sunchokes" and *"Helianthus tuberosus"*) and for "potatoes" (*"erdbar,"* or "earth pear," and *"daytshe kartofl,"* or "German potatoes").

Lewando's taxonomy of dishes probably reflects the provenance of the recipes more than their actual use. Three separate sections—"Kugels with Cholents," "Puddings," and *"Teygekhtsn"* (now "Substantial Puddings")—are devoted to more or less interchangeable puddings. Recipes in the sections *"Omletn"* ("Omelets") and *"Faynkukhns"* ("Frittatas") are largely interchangeable, as are those in the sections for "Latkes" and "Cutlets." A short section is devoted to Passover foods, but many other recipes are suitable for Passover. Cheese dumplings find their way into "Latkes," and one section is devoted simply to "Miscellaneous Dishes."

YIDDISH WORDS IN THE TEXT

I have used the Romanization of the YIVO Institute (Fania Lewando's Vilna neighbor) for all Yiddish words except those that are familiar as English words. Thus I spell the word "blintz" with a "z" because it is a common English word and "cholent" with a "ch" for the same reason. For information about specific lexical items and idioms, I am grateful to my friend Khayale Palevsky, a native of Vilna and skilled cook, and to Dr. Paul Glasser of the YIVO Institute.

Whenever possible, I have followed Lewando's paragraph breaks and punctuation. All comments in parentheses are from Fania Lewando's original text, and all editorial glosses and notes in the text are italicized and in square brackets.

EQUIPMENT AND TECHNIQUE

The techniques needed to master most of the recipes will be familiar to somewhat experienced cooks, and Lewando usually does not specify what equipment to use. The cook is instructed, for instance, to beat egg whites into a meringue, but not directed to use a whisk. Most of the equipment called for in this book (when equipment is specified at all) will be familiar. One device Lewando employs frequently is a food mill, always referred to simply as *"di mashinke,"* or "the little machine." A food mill uses a crank to turn a metal blade, pushing soft foods through the holes of a sieve, simultaneously mashing the food and straining out fibrous bits such as seeds and skin. Food mills are available in hardware and kitchen stores. In most cases, a food processor can do the job of a food mill, but you may need to peel and seed the ingredients before processing.

The coal- or wood-fired ovens available to homemakers in prewar Vilna did not have adjustable thermostats, and Lewando provides no oven temperatures except to specify on occasion a "not-too-hot oven," or a "warm oven," or a "hot oven." The recipes seem to indicate that the baking oven temperature is close to 350° Fahrenheit. A "hot oven" appears to be approximately 400°–425°, and a "warm oven," around 300°.

TO THE COOK

To make the cookbook accessible to contemporary cooks, I converted the recipes from Lewando's measurements in "decas" (decagrams) to volume measurements in cups. To convert weight to volume measurements, I weighed out each ingredient called for in each recipe, including recipes that were not tested, and then I measured the volume of the weighed amount. For instance, ten decas of raisins is two-thirds of a cup, ten decas of semolina is a rounded one-third of a cup, ten decas of uncooked rice is one-half of a cup, ten decas of cooked rice is two-thirds of a cup, and so on.

In almost all cases, you may approach the recipes with confidence that you will be delighted with the results, but with the caution that they are written in the elliptical, telegraphic style of prewar cookbooks. Though I have carefully edited all the recipes to make them usable in the contemporary kitchen, I have in most cases refrained from adding too much extra verbiage, to allow Lewando's unique voice to be heard and to resonate. Read each recipe through carefully before proceeding, understanding that the directions might be in a counterintuitive order, and that the preparation of ingredients, such as dicing or grating, may not be treated as separate, initial steps. Also, there are some recipes, such as Preserved Eggs (page 182, under "Marinated Foods"), that are worthy of interest as historical documents but that most contemporary cooks will not choose to reproduce on their own.

פעטרעשקע
Parsley

גצלצרעפקע
Cole-rape

Fania Lewando:
A Lost Treasure from Jewish Vilna

EFRAIM SICHER

Ben-Gurion University of the Negev

Known as the "Jerusalem of Lithuania," Vilna was long famous as a center of Jewish learning and culture. It had thriving communal and cultural institutions, charity organizations, and every type of secular and religious school. Vilna was a stronghold of the socialist Jewish Bund, and the Zionist organizations Po'alei Tzion, Hovevei Tzion, and Mizrakhi flourished there, too. Between the two world wars, when it was part of Poland, Vilna witnessed the heyday of Yiddish theater and, with the emergence of the Yung-Vilne movement, modernist poetry. It was home to YIVO, the institute for Yiddish studies. Eighty-five percent of Vilna's fifty-five thousand Jews declared Yiddish as their first language. Despite Vilna's economic and cultural marginalization during the interwar years, it was one of the major centers of Jewish culture in Eastern Europe before the Holocaust. And it was at Dieto-Jarska Jadłodajnia, the restaurant at 14 Niemiecka Ulica* owned by Lazar Lewando and operated by his wife, my great-aunt Fania (or, as she was known in our family, Feige)

---

* This street was known in Yiddish as Daitche Gasse; it is known in Vilnius today as Vokiečių Gatvė.

Lewando, that many of Vilna's Jewish celebrities gathered and talked about art and politics, as you can see from the excerpts from Fania's guest book that appear in the back of this book. Looking at the list of names, one can easily imagine the scintillating conversations that must have taken place at the tables—and between the tables—in the restaurant.

This was no ordinary restaurant, and Fania was no ordinary woman. In 1938, Fania Lewando published her vegetarian Yiddish cookbook, and she was well known in Vilna and beyond. She traveled to England to try to interest the food manufacturer H. J. Heinz (which had factories at Peckham and Harlesden) in her recipes, and possibly to get a job. The Yiddish press reported on a luxury cruise across the Atlantic on which Fania served as chef, accompanied by a uniformed rabbi to supervise the kosher food preparation. And besides being a businesswoman and a proponent of vegetarian Jewish cooking, Fania was also active in teaching local Jewish women the fine points of correct nutrition in her dietary school. This was a time when efforts were being made by the Vilna women's self-help movement, the *Froyen Fareyn*, to

Fania Lewando (center) teaching Jewish women about healthy diet and nutrition, Vilna, 1930s

teach women to be independent and productive, while the TOZ[*] was working to improve the overall health of the Jewish population.

Fania was born in Włocławek, in northern Poland, around 1889, to Haim Efraim (Hyman) Fiszliewicz, a fishmonger whose business often took him across the German border, and Esther-Makhalah (née Stulzaft). Fania was the second of six children (five of them girls). Her family immigrated to England in 1901 (Fania's sisters Rosa and Golda had previously left for America, but Golda rejoined the family in England), where their name was changed to Fisher. Fania remained in Poland (then still ruled by the Russian tsar) and eventually married Lazar (Eliezer) Lewando, an egg merchant who was born in Belorussia. Lazar was apparently arrested as a bourgeois capitalist when the Soviets invaded the newly independent Poland in 1920, but he managed to escape, despite being wounded in the leg. He and Fania then moved to Vilna, briefly the capital of independent Lithuania before it was annexed by Poland in 1922. The United States refused them an immigration visa on account of Lazar's leg injury, and after a second and last short visit to her family in England, Fania had to return to Vilna, where anti-Semitism was making life very difficult. Following the death in 1935 of Marshal Józef Piłsudski, supporters of the Polish National Democratic Party in Vilna spread their anti-Semitic poison. Jews were prominent in trade and finance, but many now found it hard to make a living as economic conditions worsened and Jewish businesses were nationalized or boycotted. Attacks on Jews increased, as well as on Jewish homes and stores.

With Germany's invasion of Poland and the outbreak of war in September 1939, and in accordance with the Molotov-Ribbentrop Pact, eastern Poland and the Baltic States (including Vilna) were ceded to the Soviet Union, while Germany took the rest of Poland. After a brief spell of independence, Lithuania was incorporated into the USSR on June 15, 1940. Communist rule could not have been easy for the Jews of Vilna, who relied on free trade, though some welcomed the Soviets out of fear of Germany or because of ideological conviction. Yeshivot and synagogues were closed down, and only

---

[*] Towarzystwo Ochrony Zdrowia Ludności Żydowskiej (Society for Safeguarding the Health of the Jewish Population).

a few Yiddish secular institutions were permitted to function. The Nazis invaded the USSR on June 22, 1941, and entered Vilna on June 24, followed by the *Einsatzgruppen* killing squads; as many as seventy thousand Jews were murdered in the nearby Ponary forest over the following months. On September 6–7, Vilna's Jews were confined in a ghetto. Although we do not have exact dates, we know from witnesses' accounts that Fania and Lazar were captured by Soviet soldiers while trying to flee the Nazis; they presumably perished sometime thereafter, as all trace of them was then lost.

The *Vilna Vegetarian Cookbook* is a *matzeva* (memorial) to Fania Lewando, *hy'd,* a woman who devoted her life to promoting Jewish vegetarian cuisine and educating Jewish women. It is also a testimony to the lost world of Jewish Vilna.

Fania Lewando (in the background, standing between two waitresses) with diners in her restaurant, 1930s (COURTESY OF SHELLEY SINCLAIR AND PHIL SEATON)

Briedis, Laimonas. *Vilnius: City of Strangers*. Vilnius: Baltos Lankos, 2009.

Dawidowicz, Lucy. *From That Place and Time: A Memoir, 1918–1947*. New York: W. W. Norton, 1989.

Fishman, David E. *The Rise of Modern Yiddish Culture*. Pittsburgh: University of Pittsburgh Press, 2005.

Gutman, Yisrael, et al., eds. *The Jews of Poland Between Two World Wars*. Hanover, N.H.: University Press of New England, 1989.

Katz, Dovid. *Words on Fire: The Unfinished Story of Yiddish*. Revised edition. New York: Basic Books, 2004.

Kellman, Ellen. "Creating Space for Women in Interwar Jewish Vilna: The Role of the *Froyen-farewyn*," in *Jewish Space in Central and Eastern Europe: Day-to-Day History*, ed. Jurgita Verbickienė and Larisa Lempertienė. Newcastle-upon-Tyne: Cambridge Scholars Publishing, 2007, pp. 135–42.

Klauzner, Yisrael. *Vilna, Yerushalayim Delita: Dorot Akhronim, 1881–1939*. Kibbutz Mordei Hagetaot, Israel: Ghetto Fighters House, 1983.

Marcus, Joseph. *Social and Political History of the Jews in Poland, 1919–1939*. Berlin: Mouton, 1983.

Mendelsohn, Ezra. *The Jews of East Central Europe Between the World Wars*. Bloomington: Indiana University Press, 1983.

Ran, Leyzer, ed. *Jerusalem of Lithuania: Illustrated and Documented*. New York: Vilna Album Committee, three volumes, 1974–75.

Zalkin, Mordechai. "Antisemitism in Lithuania," in *Antisemitism in Eastern Europe: History and Present in Comparison*, ed. Hans-Christian Petersen and Samuel Salzborn. Frankfurt am Main: Peter Lang, 2010, pp. 135–70.

———. "Vilnius," in *YIVO Encyclopedia of Jews in Eastern Europe*, vol. 2. New Haven, Conn.: Yale University Press, 2008, pp. 1970–77.

I would like to thank the Fisher and Skolnick families, as well as Professor Mordechai Zalkin and Aviva E. Astrinsky, for their help in preparing this essay.

פאַנני לעוואַנדאָ

וועגעטאַריש-דיעטישער
קאָבוך

400 שפּײַזן געמאַכט אויסשליסלעך פֿון גרינסן

ווילנע — 1938

Title page of the original Yiddish edition

The Vilna Vegetarian Cookbook

ברוקסעלקעס

Brussel sprouts

To the Housewife:
A Few Words and Practical Advice

It has long been established by the highest medical authorities that food made from fruits and vegetables is far healthier and more suitable for the human organism than food made from meat (the article that follows, by Dr. B. Dembski, will address this in greater detail).

We know, furthermore, that in these unhealthy times there is almost no house in which you will not find one or more family members who cannot eat meat and must follow a special vegetarian diet.

From the prophylactic point of view (that is, to protect oneself and family members from various stomach upsets and other illnesses), one must certainly make an effort to avoid meat at least three days a week.

From the humanitarian principle of *tsar baaley khayim* (not killing living creatures,[*] the principle behind the vegetarian movement), it would be desirable to replace meat with a purely vegetarian cuisine.

We hear housewives speaking among themselves, however, about there being "no meat to cook." This is a sign of how we Jews think of not eating meat as a hardship, a sign of mourning (as in the case of the nine days in memory of the destruction of the Temple).[†]

All of this has moved us to bring out this first vegetarian cookbook in

---

[*] The literal translation of this Hebrew phrase is "causing living creatures to suffer." —*Ed.*

[†] The nine days leading up to the annual commemoration of the destruction of both the First and Second Temples in Jerusalem, on the ninth day of the month of Av, are considered days of semimourning, during which meat is not eaten. —*Ed.*

Yiddish, with more than four hundred nourishing recipes (from various vegetables and fruits), to promote the vegetarian cuisine in general, and to serve in particular housewives who must maintain a dietetic kitchen.

One must strictly observe the following directions:

1. *The produce must be of the best quality.* There is only a small difference in price between the best and worst produce, but in cooking there is a great difference, in taste as well as in nutrition.

2. *One must use clean utensils.* If they are enameled, one must make sure there are no scratches, because this is harmful to health.

3. *Use only centrifuge butter for frying, baking, and other cooking.*[*] This butter is uncultured, unlike peasant butter, and it does not burn while frying. It is not true that hand-churned butter is richer. The machine is more efficient than the hands.

4. *Throw nothing out; everything can be made into food.* For example, don't throw out the water in which you have cooked mushrooms or green peas; it can be used for various soups. Don't throw out the vegetables used to make a vegetable broth. You can make various foods from them, as is shown in this cookbook.

5. *Prepare everything precisely as instructed in the recipes, and do not rely on others.* All these foods can be easily made, because I have tested each recipe several times.

I have the fullest satisfaction in the knowledge that my cookbook is practical and that it will be very useful to every housewife in her daily life.

F. LEWANDO

---

[*] The equivalent today would be clarified butter. —*Ed.*

Why Are Fruits and Vegetables
So Important for the Organism?

The main elements of our nutrition are proteins, fats, carbohydrates, minerals, and vitamins. It was long widely believed that the only real foods were the proteins and fats from animals, and that fruits and vegetables were no more than snacks, which, though tasty, were useless, or, according to some, even harmful. Modern science, however, has revealed the falsity of these beliefs.

Let us briefly review the components of vegetables and fruits. They are rich in water, in general up to 80 percent. The defenders of meat eating used to invoke this richness in water frequently as a sign of the uselessness of fruits. One must, however, remember that the water that fruits and vegetables contain cannot be compared to ordinary water from a well or faucet. First of all, it is entirely free of bacteria; secondly, this water contains sugar, minerals, organic acids, fragrant and flavorful material, and various enzymes.

Fruits and vegetables contain many carbohydrates—in particular, many sugars.

Sugars are the carbohydrates most easily metabolized and absorbed directly into the blood, and do not require complex processing, as do starches, for instance. Fruits and vegetables contain significant amounts of cellulose, which promotes cleaning out the colon and regularity.

Fruits and vegetables contain the enzymes that assist the separation of complicated compounds into simple parts necessary for the organism to make what it needs. The fragrant and flavorful materials stimulate the appetite, help with the distribution of gastric juices, and activate the membranes of the colon and kidneys.

The skins of fruits and berries are especially important for the digestion process. This is particularly the case with blueberries.

Minerals are very important. In the past they were unknown and undervalued. Now we know that without a constant supply of minerals our bodies cannot be healthy.

Almost all important minerals are present in fruits and vegetables; most important, the percentage of alkalinity is significantly greater than acidity. This is why they work so well as cleansers of the system. The regular use of vegetables and fruits protects the body from various diseases that are caused by poor elimination—obesity, gout, and so on. It is not unusual for doctors to prescribe a fruit cure for these diseases.

Fruits and berries are also recommended for fever sufferers. When one has a fever, the body is not building new tissue, and proteins are not needed. They are in fact a harmful, heavy ballast.

On the contrary, the body needs fuel, and as we have seen, fruits and vegetables are rich in easily burned fuel. In addition, the fever sufferer needs alkaline material to neutralize the waste products he is producing, particularly phosphorous acid, and alkaline salt, calcium, potassium, and sodium are plentiful in fruits and vegetables. Potassium and calcium also have the ability to rid the body of excess water; they are diuretics. And fruits are rich in vitamins, without which the body cannot survive.

Fruits must be well chewed and entirely consumed, including the peel. One must, however, not eat the pits, such as those in plums and cherries. They contain a toxic acid that could be poisonous if consumed in large quantities.

Fruits are more useful if eaten raw. It is enough to place them in a strainer and pour hot water over them.

One must remember that when one eats lots of fruit one needs only a small amount of meat and eggs; this is very helpful to the organism.

Vegetables are divided into various categories. The main groups are the following: (1) leafy (lettuce, spinach, sorrel, pea pods, various kinds of cabbage, asparagus, and green onions); (2) root vegetables (radishes, rutabagas, and turnips); (3) herb vegetables (onions, horseradish, garlic, caraway, etc.); (4) fruit vegetables (cucumbers, tomatoes, eggplant, squash, and melons).

Most vegetables are very rich in water (80 to 95 percent). The water within vegetables is distinguished by the same useful properties as the water within fruits—it is free from all kinds of bacteria, and contains soluble forms of many useful elements. The water within vegetables does not impede blood circulation. On the contrary, thanks to the potassium and calcium that it contains, it frees the tissues from excess moisture that has accumulated in them, and also from other hidden waste products. It works as a solvent, or cleanser of the body.

It has been noted that rabbits and guinea pigs, who live on fresh grass and vegetables, never want to drink. When, on the other hand, they switch to dry fodder, they can't go a day without water. It is the same with a human being. If his nourishment is mostly from fruits and vegetables, he feels almost no thirst. With meat foods, salted and spiced, he drinks lots of fluids.

The most important thing about vegetables is their richness in minerals and vitamins.

Vegetables contain complexes that are very easy for our bodies to break down—minerals that go into the makeup of the juices and tissues of our body and that must be constantly renewed. Vegetables have significantly more alkalinity than acidity, which is important because the majority of harmful waste matter from the body causes an acid reaction, and alkalinity is necessary in order to neutralize the waste matter and make it harmless. This is how vegetables work to freshen, cleanse, and renew the organism.

It has long been observed that people who live for lengthy periods of time on dried foods and preserved meats (such as sailors on long voyages or soldiers in the trenches) would become ill in great numbers from scurvy. This illness disappeared without any medication when they added even a small amount of vegetables or fruit juice to their diet.

The green leaves of vegetables contain a coloring agent—chlorophyll. It catches the sun's energy and collects it like a battery. With its help, the body carries out a series of complicated chemical reactions. For instance, it catches the carbon dioxide from the air (the harmful gas we exhale), deconstructs it, returns the oxygen to the air, and builds starch from the carbon. Chlorophyll helps build both vitamin and mineral complexes.

Chlorophyll aids the renewal of blood, the replenishing of blood cells, and the collection of hemoglobin. It helps in combating anemia, regulates metabolism, and helps renew the organism.

The majority of vegetables are eaten cooked; many of them contain carbohydrates in the form of starches, which can be eaten only when cooked. Under no circumstances should one discard the water in which vegetables have been cooked: prepare a soup or purée from it.

DR. B. DEMBSKI

(An excerpt from Dr. Dembski's article in Folksgezunt*)*[*]

---

[*] A periodical, published in Yiddish in Vilna from 1923 to 1940, that contained articles about health and nutrition. —*Ed.*

Vegetarianism as a Jewish Movement

The idea of vegetarianism and its promulgation originated in France, but the first association for vegetarians was established in England in 1847. Shortly thereafter, a whole series of vegetarian societies sprang up in America and Central Europe. They believed that the only natural food for people comes from plants.

The followers of this philosophy are called "vegetarians," and their subject "vegetarianism" (from the Latin *vegetare,* to grow).*

There is no doubt that nourishing oneself with plants can maintain life, strength, and health to the same extent as a mixed diet. Many vegetables—such as lentils, chickpeas, beans, and so on—contain more necessary proteins than many meats. The fact that many peasants and workers who cannot afford meat are (like it or not) vegetarians shows that vegetables can maintain the productivity needed for their work. Furthermore, in China and Japan, meat is seldom eaten, and most people subsist on vegetables, rice, and so on.

Because of the natural increase in the world's population, the gradual expansion in agriculture, and the continuing development of industry, mankind will be driven to vegetarianism in the not-too-distant future.

As we can see, vegetarianism has solid scientific as well as social, cultural, and historic justification.

To the scientific arguments, one can add the comparison of people to related animals such as monkeys, who have similar teeth and digestive systems, and who subsist in the wild exclusively on plants, mostly fruit.

---

* Actually, *vegetare,* in Late Latin, meant "enliven." In medieval Latin, *vegetabilis* meant "growing." —*Ed.*

Vegetarians call their theory the study of a life suited to nature. They point out that very few of them are sickly, and they say that killing living creatures is against human nature. They are fully convinced that people will eventually transform themselves from being necrophagous—that is, scavengers (according to them)—into fruit-and-vegetable eaters.

The first and most famous vegetarian association was founded, as stated above, in 1847, in Manchester, the Vegetarian Society; it has many branches throughout Great Britain and North America. It publishes a great deal of promotional material, including books and journals. Germany and Switzerland have vegetarian societies, as do Italy, Spain, France, and Poland. In England, Austria, Germany, and Switzerland, there are hotels with special vegetarian kitchens.

It is worth noting that, according to the Bible, the first permitted foods were plants. In Genesis 1:29 it is written: "And God said, 'I give you all seed-bearing grasses that grow on the earth and all trees that bear fruit and this shall be for you to eat.' " Meat became permitted only after the flood, when there were not yet any new plants to eat.

By the way, here are the names of a few famous personalities known to be vegetarians: Leo Tolstoy, Romain Rolland, Gandhi, George Bernard Shaw, and Ilya Repin, among many others.

BEN-ZION KIT[*]

---

[*] This was a pen name for two of the people listed in the last paragraph as famous vegetarians: Romain Rolland (1866–1944), French author and professor of music at the Sorbonne, won the Nobel Prize for Literature in 1915; Ilya Repin (1844–1930) was a leading Russian naturalist painter and sculptor. —Ed.

Vitamins

People cannot live without vitamins. Vegetables have the most vitamins. There are five vitamins:

Vitamin A aids growth and strengthens the bones.

Vitamin B aids growth and digestion.

Vitamin C prevents scurvy.

Vitamin D aids metabolism.

Vitamin E prevents rickets.

Foods that contain vitamins A, B, C, D, and E: green spinach, raw carrot juice, raw and cooked tomatoes, raw carrots.

Foods that contain vitamins A, B, C, and D: cooked spinach, red and white cabbage, lettuce, and turnips.

Foods that contain vitamins B, C, D, and a little of A: cauliflower, green beans, string beans, cooked potatoes, and oranges.

Foods that contain vitamins B, C, and D: onions and grapes.

Foods that contain vitamins A, B, and D: cooked carrots.

Eggs have A, B, and C.

Cream has A, B, and D.

Butter has A.

סאַלאַט
Salad

Salads

MAYONNAISE PROVENÇAL

Place 2 soft-boiled and 3 raw egg yolks in a bowl, sprinkle with some sugar and salt, mix well, and gradually beat in 1 cup [vegetable] oil by the teaspoonful, beating continually with a wooden spoon, until it is all absorbed. While beating, dribble in the juice of 1 lemon (if you want to yield more mayonnaise, add more oil and more lemon). Mayonnaise is suitable for all salads.

SALAD WITH MAYONNAISE PROVENÇAL

Dice 1 small cooked potato, 3 sour pickled cucumbers, 4 hard-boiled eggs, 10 Marinated Mushrooms [see page 181], 2 cooked carrots, and 1 cooked celery root. Add to this ¼ cup cooked green peas, half a cup cooked beans, the juice of 1 lemon, and some salt. Mix this with Mayonnaise Provençal made with 2 cups oil [that is 2 recipes of the mayonnaise].

> *[White beans, such as Great Northern, navy, and cannellini, work well for this recipe.—Ed.]*

GREEN SALAD WITH MAYONNAISE PROVENÇAL

Cut up a large bunch of washed salad greens, and add 3 diced hard-boiled eggs, 1 diced cucumber, and 1 sectioned lemon. Mix well, dress with Mayonnaise Provençal, and serve immediately.

TOMATOES STUFFED WITH SALADE PROVENÇAL

Cut 6 good large firm tomatoes in half, hollow them out, sprinkle the shells with a bit of salt, and fill with Salad with Mayonnaise Provençal. Serve with slices of lemon, and sprinkle with [chopped fresh] dill.

TOMATO SALAD

Cut 2 firm tomatoes, 1 cucumber, and 1 onion into thin slices. Lay them in a salad bowl, sprinkle with a bit of salt, pepper, and [chopped fresh] dill and parsley, and squeeze in the juice of ½ lemon. Drizzle in 3 tablespoons [olive] oil.

SALAD OF MARINATED PEARS

Cut into small pieces 6 Marinated Pears [see page 180], 15 Marinated Mushrooms [see page 181], 1 orange, 1 apple, and 3 hard-boiled eggs. Add ¼ cup cooked green peas. Mix well, and dress with Mayonnaise Provençal.

SALAD OF SAUERKRAUT WITH MARINATED *BOROVKES* MUSHROOMS

Mix 1 pound Sauerkraut [see page 182] with 1 thinly sliced onion, 10 diced Marinated Mushrooms [see page 181], and a bit of salt. Mix and dress with ½ cup [olive] oil. Eat with freshly cooked potatoes.

[The borovkes (borowki) *called for in this and many of Fania's recipes are porcini or cèpes, deeply flavored mushrooms favored in Polish cookery.—Ed.]*

EGGPLANT APPETIZER

Broil 2 large purple eggplants, and remove the charred skins. Sauté 2 [chopped] onions and 3 tomatoes in [olive] oil. Grind the sautéed vegetables with a bit of challah that has been soaked in vinegar. Add this to the broiled eggplant pulp and chop well. Then mix with salt, [chopped fresh] dill, and ½ cup of the best oil. Serve decorated with sliced tomatoes, cucumbers, and dill.

VITAMIN SALAD WITH RAW CABBAGE

Thinly slice 2 pounds raw cabbage, salt it, and allow to rest 1 hour in a bowl, weighted with a smaller bowl. Squeeze out the liquid, add the juice of 2 lemons and ½ cup [olive] oil, and mix well. Serve sprinkled with [chopped] green onions.

SALADE VINAIGRETTE

Boil 2 pounds potatoes and roast 1 pound beets separately, in their skins. Peel and thinly slice the vegetables. Add 1 thinly sliced Spanish onion and 2 thinly sliced lemons. Add salt and [chopped fresh] dill, and mix well. Serve dressed with [olive] oil and sprinkled with [chopped fresh] dill and green onions.

POTATO SALAD

Cook 2 pounds of potatoes in their skins. When they are cool, peel them and cut into thin slices. Add 1 [thinly sliced] Spanish onion, 2 thinly sliced peeled lemons, and some salt, and mix well. Dress with ¼ cup [olive] oil, and sprinkle with [chopped fresh] green onions and dill.

FRENCH SALAD OF COOKED CARROTS AND GREEN PEAS

Cut 1 pound cooked carrots into slices, and add ¼ cup cooked dried green peas, 2 peeled and thinly sliced lemons (without the seeds), and salt, and mix. Dress with ½ cup [olive] oil, and serve sprinkled with [chopped] green onion. In summertime, you can make this with fresh peas.

RADISH SALAD

Cut up a large bunch of salad greens, 3 apples, 3 hard-boiled eggs, 10 radishes, and 1 lemon. Add some sliced green onions and salt. Dress with ½ cup [olive] oil and mix lightly. Make this immediately before serving.

VITAMIN SALAD WITH CARROTS

Peel 1 pound carrots, and grate on a box grater. Sprinkle with 1 tablespoon sugar and the juice of 1½ lemons. Allow to rest in a bowl under a weight, in a cool place, for 2 hours, before serving.

FRESH CUCUMBER SALAD

Thinly slice 3 fresh cucumbers and sprinkle with salt. Allow to rest under a weight for 10 minutes. In the meantime, squeeze the juice from 1 lemon, add 2 tablespoons sugar, and mix with 1 cup sour cream. Squeeze out and discard the accumulated liquid from the cucumbers, add [chopped fresh] dill, and mix with the prepared dressing. Serve with fried potatoes.

SALAD OF MARINATED CORNICHONS
WITH MARINATED MUSHROOMS

Dice 10 marinated cornichons (small cucumbers) and 10 Marinated Mushrooms [see page 181]. Add ¼ cup cooked green peas and 2 diced hard-boiled eggs, and mix well. Serve sprinkled with a diced green onion or Spanish onion.

BEAN SALAD

Soak [any type of dried] beans in salted water for a few hours, and cook in the same water until soft. Drain the water, allow the beans to cool, and then add the juice of 1 lemon. Sprinkle with diced onions or scallions, and dress with [olive] oil.

STUFFED TOMATO APPETIZER

Scoop the soft insides from 2 pounds small firm tomatoes. Sauté them in oil with 2 minced onions. Meanwhile, grate 1 small carrot, 1 small parsley root [a parsnip can be substituted], and 1 small celery root. Sauté the grated vegetables in oil. Mix everything together, and fill the empty tomatoes. To serve, sprinkle with [chopped fresh] dill and scallions, and surround with fresh lettuce.

RED CABBAGE SALAD

Shred and boil 1 pound red cabbage in a bit of water [enough to cover cabbage]. Drain the water, and add the juice of 2 lemons, ¼ cup cooked beans [any type of canned beans would be fine], 2 diced pickled cucumbers, 3 Antonovka apples [or any tart, crisp apple, such as Cortland, Jonathan, or Winesap], 4 hard-boiled eggs, salt, and 2 tablespoons sugar. Mix well, and dress with ¾ cup [olive] oil or mayonnaise (see Mayonnaise Provençal, page 14).

CHEESE SALAD

Mash up ½ pound [one 8-ounce package] farmer cheese. Add salt, pepper, a diced green onion, and 1 cup sour cream, and mix well. Eat with black bread.

CREAM WITH CHEESE

Crumble ½ pound [one 8-ounce package] farmer cheese. Add salt, pepper, and 1 cup [sour] cream, and mix.

SALAD WITH LEMON SAUCE (MISERIA)

Mash 2 hard-boiled egg yolks with 2 tablespoons sugar. Squeeze in the juice of 1 lemon. Add a large handful of lettuce leaves, 1 [sliced] cucumber, some diced green onion, some sliced radishes, a little [chopped fresh] dill and salt, and also 2 hard-boiled egg whites. Dress with 1 cup sour cream, and mix well. Eat with new potatoes.

VITAMIN SALAD

Put a small handful of lettuce leaves, 2 diced hard-boiled eggs, 6 diced radishes, some salt, [chopped fresh] dill, and [sliced] green onion into a glass salad bowl. Squeeze in the juice of 1 lemon, dress with ½ cup [olive] oil, and mix well. Prepare this salad just before eating.

APPLE AND HORSERADISH SALAD

Grate [1 ounce] horseradish, sprinkle with [¼ teaspoon] salt and [½ teaspoon] sugar, and add 2 [medium] apples, grated. Squeeze in the juice of 1 lemon, and dress with [1 tablespoon] [olive] oil.

> *[The intensity of this salad will depend on the amount of horseradish and the size and sweetness of the apples. The recipe is a good accompaniment to any of the cutlets or latkes and is perfect for Passover.—Ed.]*

VITAMIN SALAD (ANOTHER ONE)

Grate 2 raw carrots, 1 celery root, 1 small turnip, and a radish. Add ¼ cup shredded horseradish and some salt. Mix everything together well, and place in a salad bowl. Add the juice of 2 lemons and ½ cup [olive] oil, and mix well. Serve sprinkled with diced scallions.

APPLE SALAD

Dice 1 pound raw apples, 2 pickled cucumbers, and 2 hard-boiled eggs. Then grate 1 celery root. Mix everything with Mayonnaise Provençal (see the recipe on page 14). Serve with thinly sliced Spanish onion.

ORANGE SALAD

Steam ¼ cup green peas. Cut into small pieces 3 oranges, 2 large apples, 1½ cups walnuts, 2 hard-boiled eggs, and 2 cooked carrots. Mix everything with mayonnaise (see the recipe for Mayonnaise Provençal on page 14).

LEEK APPETIZER

Cut 3 large leeks and 2 Spanish onions into small pieces, and sauté in butter. Add 3 diced hard-boiled eggs, 6 tablespoons butter, 4 tablespoons bread crumbs, 3 diced scallions, and [chopped fresh] dill. Add 2 raw eggs and some salt, and mix well. Melt 2 tablespoons butter in a pot, and add the leek mixture. Cover well, and bake ½ hour. Serve sprinkled with dill.

[For best results, sauté the leeks and onions slowly over a low flame. It will take about 20 minutes. None of the recipes in this collection specifies an oven temperature, for the simple reason that temperature in the wood or coal ovens of that era could not be easily adjusted. A moderate oven of about 350° F works for most of the recipes, unless otherwise specified.—Ed.]

TOMATO APPETIZER

Push 6 cooked tomatoes through a sieve [to create a tomato purée]. Cut 6 bread rolls into small cubes, and sauté in butter. Put them in a pot, pour the puréed tomatoes over them, sprinkle with salt and pepper, dot with 6 tablespoons butter, and bake ½ hour.

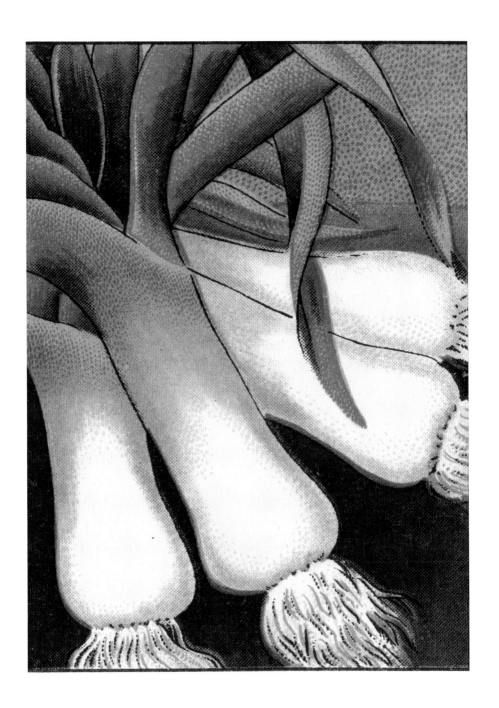

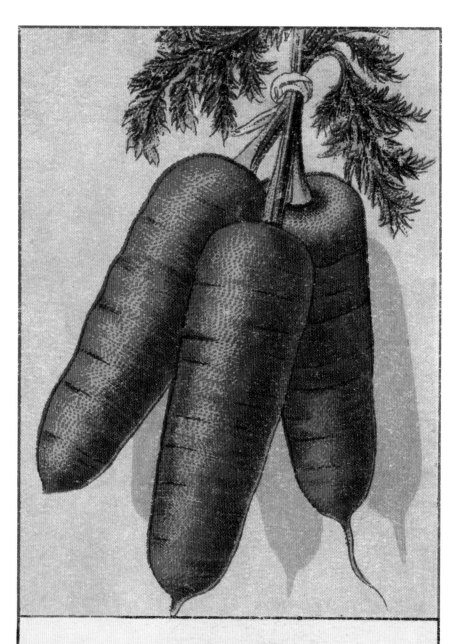

מ ע ר ן

Carrot

Soups

Mix 1 beaten egg with some salt, sugar, and 1 tablespoon [vegetable] oil. Add ¾ cup flour, and mix well to make a light dough. Cut the dough into small cubes. Heat ¾ cup oil in a deep skillet. Add the dough pieces, and sauté until brown.

PURÉED CARROT SOUP

Cook 2 pounds carrots, 5 potatoes, and 1 celery root in 1 quart water until soft. Purée the vegetables, and return them to the broth. Add 1 cup fresh peas, 1 head cooked, cut-up cauliflower, and 1 quart milk, and simmer 25 minutes, making sure it does not burn. Then add a roux made from 1½ teaspoons melted butter and 1 tablespoon flour, 1 tablespoon sugar, and some salt, and cook 5 more minutes.

VEGETABLE SOUP

Bring 2 quarts water to the boil. Add ½ cup pearl barley [and cook about 20 minutes]. Add 2 tablespoons butter, 1 [head] cauliflower cut in pieces, 1 bunch (1 pound) carrots cut in pieces, 1 pound shelled peas, a little [chopped] fresh parsley, 4 or 5 new potatoes, and 1 [cut-up] kohlrabi, and cook everything until soft, about 20 minutes. Make a roux from 1½ teaspoons melted butter and 1 tablespoon flour, and add to the soup. Salt to taste, and cook 15 minutes more. When serving, sprinkle each bowl with [chopped fresh] parsley and dill.

BEER SOUP

Bring one [12-ounce] bottle of beer to the boil. Beat together 6 egg yolks, 2 tablespoons sugar, 1 tablespoon honey, and some salt. While beating, gradually stir in the hot beer, and return to heat, stirring until all ingredients are well combined. Do not bring to boil. Eat this with toasted rolls and Dutch [Edam or Gouda] cheese. You can also eat it cold.

LENTIL SOUP

Pick over 1 pound (about 2 cups) lentils. Rinse them, and then soak in 2 cups water for 3 hours. [Drain and set aside.] In a large pot, bring to the boil 6 cups water, and add 2 small celery roots, 2 ounces dried mushrooms, 4 parsley roots [parsnips can be substituted], 4 leeks, and 4 carrots, and cook 1 hour. Strain out the vegetables, pour the broth over the lentils, and cook until soft, about 30 minutes. In the meantime, add 3 cut-up potatoes, the 4 cooked carrots, and Soup Nuts made with 1 egg [1 recipe; see opposite page]. Sauté 2 minced onions in ½ cup melted butter, and add to the soup. Cook about 10 minutes longer. Sprinkle with [chopped fresh] dill and parsley.

MUSHROOM SOUP

In a large pot, bring 2 quarts water to a boil. Add 2 celery roots, 4 leeks, 4 parsley roots [parsnips can be substituted], and 4 carrots. Cook ½ hour, and strain out the vegetables. Add to the broth 1 cup sliced mushrooms that were earlier washed and sautéed. Add 1 cup green peas, and cook 1 hour. Then sprinkle in ½ cup farfel [noodle barley that has been cooked according to package directions]; 2 of the cooked carrots, mashed; 2 minced onions that have been sautéed in ½ cup melted butter; salt and pepper to taste; and a bit of [chopped fresh] dill and parsley, and cook about 10 minutes longer.

[Fania provides a noodle barley recipe on page 87.—Ed.]

POTATO SOUP

Cook 2 celery roots, 2 carrots, and 2 parsley roots [parsnips can be substituted] in 2 quarts water for ½ hour. Add 4 pounds potatoes, cut into thin slices, and cook until the potatoes are soft, about 20 minutes. Purée the soup by putting the vegetables through a food mill. Meanwhile, grate 3 onions, add 1 tablespoon flour, some pepper, and a few bay leaves, and sauté in ½ cup melted butter. Add to the soup, and cook about 10 minutes more. Serve sprinkled with fresh dill.

SAGO SOUP

In a large pot, bring 2 quarts water to the boil. Add 2 celery roots, 2 parsley roots [parsnips can be substituted], 2 carrots, 2 leeks, and 1 ounce dried mushrooms. Cook for 1 hour. Then strain and add ¼ cup of the best sago to the clear broth. Mash the cooked vegetables, except for the parsley root, and add to the soup. Meanwhile, cut 2 potatoes into long thin strips, blanch in boiling salted water, and add to the soup. Simmer ½ hour, stirring frequently so it does not burn. Heat ½ cup butter, and sauté 2 diced onions and 1 tablespoon flour. Add the roux to the soup, cook 10 minutes, and salt to taste. Eat with toasted rolls. You can also add 1 tablespoon sour cream to each bowl.

[Sago is a starch extracted from the spongy center of the stem of the sago palm tree. It is used as a thickener in recipes, and although tapioca has a slightly different texture, it is an acceptable substitute—use ¼ cup tapioca pearls in this recipe.—Ed.]

FRENCH SOUP

In 2 quarts water, cook 2 small celery roots, 1 parsley root [a parsnip can be substituted], 4 carrots, 3 leeks, and 1 ounce dried mushrooms for 1 hour, and strain. In another pot, steam ¼ cup green peas, and add to the broth. Cut up 1 head of Italian cabbage (or regular cabbage or cauliflower) [and add to the broth]. Mash 1 of the cooked carrots, 1 cooked celery root, and the cooked mushrooms, and then add to the soup along with 3 julienne-cut potatoes. Salt to taste, and cook about 30 minutes. Make Soup Nuts with 1 egg [see page 24]. Sauté 2 diced onions in ½ cup melted butter. Add to the soup with the Soup Nuts, and cook about 10 minutes more.

OATMEAL SOUP

Simmer 1 ounce dried mushrooms, 3 tablespoons butter, 1 parsley root [a parsnip can be substituted], 1 celery root, 2 leeks, and 2 carrots in 4 cups water for 1 hour. Then strain out the vegetables, and add to the broth 1 cup whole oats, the cooked carrots, mashed, and another 2 tablespoons butter, and cook another hour. In the meantime, make a roux with 1½ teaspoons melted butter and 1 tablespoon flour. Whisk into the soup. Serve with 1 tablespoon sweet cream and croutons (dried bits of bread-roll cubes).

MUSHROOM BROTH WITH NOODLES

Soak 3 ounces dried mushrooms in 2 quarts water overnight. The next day, add 2 carrots, 2 celery roots, 2 parsley roots [parsnips can be substituted], 2 leeks (or 2 onions), and one small, cut-up white cabbage. Simmer everything for 2 hours, and then strain. Mince 1 large onion, sauté in ½ cup melted butter with 1 tablespoon flour, and whisk into the strained soup. Cook for ½ hour, and strain once again. Serve with some noodles in each bowl (cook the noodles separately, following package directions).

CAULIFLOWER SOUP WITH NEW POTATOES

Cook ½ cup pearl barley in 2 quarts water with 4 tablespoons butter [following package directions]. Add 1 bunch diced carrots; 1 diced large head cauliflower; 1 pound new potatoes; and a little [chopped fresh] parsley; and cook until soft, about 30 minutes. Make a roux with 1 tablespoon flour and 1½ teaspoons melted butter, and add to the soup. Serve with 1 tablespoon sweet cream and a bit of [chopped fresh] dill.

ALMOND SOUP

Heat 6 cups milk with 1 celery root, 1 onion, 4 tablespoons finely ground blanched almonds, and 6 finely ground blanched bitter almonds, plus 1 teaspoon salt. Simmer slowly over a low flame for 1 hour. Remove the celery root and onion. Make a roux with 1 tablespoon flour and 1½ teaspoons melted butter, and whisk into the soup. Remove from heat, and add 1 cup sweet cream [optional]. Serve with croutons.

[To blanch almonds, pour hot water over them and allow them to cool before removing their skins. Packaged blanched almonds are much less flavorful.—Ed.]

[Because of what we now know about their toxicity, the use of raw bitter almonds is questionable. An acceptable substitute would be ¼ teaspoon almond extract.—Ed.]

FINE SEMOLINA SOUP

Bring 1 cup fine semolina [to a boil] in 3 cups milk; then simmer, stirring frequently until consistency of porridge. Add ½ cup butter and some salt, and cook an additional 5 minutes.

SOUR CREAM SOUP

Cook 1 celery root, 1 parsley root [a parsnip can be substituted], and 2 carrots in 1 quart water for 1 hour, and then strain. Meanwhile, lightly toast 4 pieces of white bread to dry them out. Place the pieces of bread in a pan with 4 tablespoons melted butter, and leave them long enough for the dried bread to soak up the butter. Beat 2 eggs together with 2 cups sour cream, and whisk into the strained soup. Pour the soup over the toasted, buttered bread. Cook, stirring occasionally, until it is just about to return to the boil, and add a bit of salt.

JERUSALEM ARTICHOKE SOUP

Cook 2 pounds cut-up Jerusalem artichokes in salted water for about 20 minutes, drain, and either push through a sieve or purée in a food processor. Add 1 quart milk, 1 tablespoon butter, and some salt, and cook for 20 more minutes. Before serving, whisk 2 egg yolks with ½ cup sour cream, pour into the soup, and mix well.

SPLIT PEA SOUP

Cook 1 pound split peas in 2½ quarts water with 1 celery root, 1 parsley root [a parsnip can be substituted], and 3 carrots. Stir a few times while cooking so the peas do not burn. When the peas are soft, after about 1 hour, remove the vegetables and either push the peas through a sieve or purée in a food processor. Add milk to taste to the purée. Then grate 1 onion and sauté in 7 tablespoons melted butter with 1 tablespoon flour. Mix this into the soup, and cook about 10 minutes more, stirring occasionally so it does not burn. Serve with rusks.

> *[Rusk is a dry, twice-baked bread. Zwieback, biscotti, and melba toast are all varieties of rusk.—Ed.]*

SUMMER SQUASH SOUP

Put 1 celery root, 2 parsley roots [parsnips can be substituted], and 3 pounds chopped summer squash in a pot with 3 cups water, and cook ½ hour. Then push through a sieve or purée in a food processor, add 4 cups milk and some sugar [and some salt and pepper], and continue to cook for about 10 minutes. Meanwhile, sauté 1 tablespoon flour in ½ cup melted butter. Pour into the soup, and cook a few minutes more.

RICE AND MUSHROOM SOUP

Combine 2 ounces unrinsed dried porcini mushrooms, 2 celery roots, 2 parsley roots [parsnips can be substituted], 5 leeks, and 4 carrots in a pot with 2 quarts water. Cook 1 hour, and then strain. Cut up the cooked mushrooms, 1 of the celery roots, and 2 of the carrots, and return to the broth. Add ½ cup rice, and cook until the rice is soft, about 15 minutes. Meanwhile, bring 3 diced potatoes and 1 can of beans to a boil [separately, in boiling water], add to the soup, and continue cooking until everything is soft, about 10 minutes. Sauté 2 grated or diced onions with 1 tablespoon flour in ½ cup plus 2 tablespoons melted butter and some salt, and add to the soup, allowing everything to cook together for another 10 to 15 minutes.

[Any type of dried mushrooms may be substituted. White beans, such as Great Northern, navy, and cannellini, work well for this recipe.—Ed.]

CHICKPEA SOUP WITH FARFEL

After soaking them overnight, cook 1 pound whole dried chickpeas [in boiling water] until soft, about 1½ hours. At the same time, combine 2 parsley roots [parsnips can be substituted], 1 onion, 4 carrots, 4 leeks, and 2 celery roots in 2 quarts water, and cook for 1 hour. Then strain, and add the [strained] chickpeas, along with some salt and pepper. Meanwhile, make thin farfel with 1 egg, and add to the soup. Then sauté 2 grated onions in 10 tablespoons melted butter until brown, add to the soup, and cook a little longer, about 10 minutes. Serve with finely minced [fresh] parsley.

[Fania provides a farfel recipe on page 87. Commercial noodle barley (either plain or toasted) can be used. Follow package directions for preparation.—Ed.]

PRUNE BUTTER *(POVIDL)* SOUP

Simmer 2 cups prune butter with 6 cups water for 10 minutes, adding sugar to taste. Serve with 1 tablespoon of sour cream in each dish. You can eat this with rusks or rolls.

[See note for Split Pea Soup, page 29.—Ed.]

CRANBERRY SOUP

Purée a pound of cranberries in a food mill or food processor, strain through a fine sieve, and add water to get 6 cups juice. Combine with 2 cups sugar, the zest of 1 lemon, and 1 tablespoon jam, and cook for 10 minutes. Meanwhile, sauté 1 tablespoon flour in 4 tablespoons melted butter, and stir into the soup. Add two diced apples, and cook a little longer, about 10 minutes, making sure the apples do not overcook. Serve with 1 tablespoon sour cream in each dish. Eat this with cheesecake.

PLUM SOUP WITH APPLES AND PEARS

Put 1 pound each of fresh [pitted] plums *(vengerkes)*, [seeded] apples, and [seeded] pears into a pot with 2 quarts water. Cook until soft, about 15 minutes, and push the pulp through a sieve or purée in a food processor. Add 1½ cups sugar, and continue cooking for about 10 minutes. Serve with 1 tablespoon sour cream in each dish. You can eat this with mashed potatoes.

PRUNE SOUP

Remove the pits from ½ pound prunes. Add 2 ounces dried apples and sugar to taste. Mix everything together in a pot with 6 cups water, and cook 1½ hours. Serve with 1 tablespoon sweet cream in each dish. Eat this with mashed potatoes or rusks.

[See note for Split Pea Soup, page 29.—Ed.]

APPLE SOUP (APPLESAUCE)

Peel and dice 4 pounds Antonovka apples [or any tart, crisp apples, such as Cortland, Jonathan, or Winesap], and cook ½ hour. Push through a sieve, add ¾ cup sugar, and cook a bit more, about 10 minutes. Serve with 1 tablespoon sour cream in each dish. Eat this with rusks. You may also eat this soup cold.

[See note for Split Pea Soup, page 29.—Ed.]

RHUBARB SOUP

Trim and slice 4 pounds rhubarb, and cook for ½ hour in 2 quarts water. Strain, and add 2 cups sugar and the zest of 1 lemon to the broth. Continue to cook for another ½ hour, and then chill. Serve with 1 tablespoon sour cream in each dish. You can eat this with new potatoes.

APRICOT SOUP

Cook 2 pounds apricots for ½ hour in 6 cups water and remove the pits. Push through a sieve, or purée in a food processor. Add sugar to taste, and add 1 tablespoon sour cream to each dish before serving. You can eat this cold. Serve with mashed potatoes.

COLD CHERRY SOUP

Cook 2 pounds black cherries in 2 quarts water for ½ hour, remove the pits, and push through a sieve or purée in a food processor. Add sugar to taste, and allow to cool. Serve with 1 tablespoon good sour cream in each dish. Eat with cheesecake or with potatoes.

COLD BLUEBERRY SOUP

Cook 4 pints blueberries in 6 cups water for ½ hour, then push through a fine sieve or purée in a food processor, add sugar to taste, and allow to cool. Serve with 1 tablespoon sour cream in each dish. Eat this with potatoes or rusks.

[See note for Split Pea Soup, page 29.—Ed.]

ROLL SOUP

Crumble 2 French bread rolls into a bowl. Add 3 tablespoons butter and some salt. Pour on 1 cup boiling water, and cover tightly for 5 minutes before serving.

[The rolls in Vilna must have been much smaller. This soup can be made with one roll.—Ed.]

CABBAGE SOUP WITH MILK

Grate 1 celery root, 2 carrots, and 1 parsley root [a parsnip can be substituted]. Combine with 12 ounces (about ½ head) shredded cabbage, and blanch everything in boiling water to reduce the bitterness [discard this first water]. Put it all in a pot, add 3 diced potatoes, some salt, and 2 cups water, and cook until soft, about 10 minutes. Then pour in 2 cups milk, and cook a little longer, about 10 minutes. Meanwhile, sauté 1 tablespoon flour in 10 tablespoons melted butter, stir into the soup, and cook an additional 10 minutes. When serving, add 1 tablespoon sweet cream to each dish.

POTATO SOUP WITH MILK

Wash and peel 2 pounds potatoes, slice thinly, and cook in boiling water for 10 minutes. Then add the cooked potatoes to 4 cups scalded milk, along with 2 thinly sliced onions, ½ cup butter, and salt (whoever uses pepper can also add pepper), and simmer until soft, about 10 minutes, stirring occasionally so it does not burn.

FARINA SOUP WITH MILK

Sprinkle ½ cup farina into a saucepan with 4 cups cold milk, and cook, stirring constantly, until it begins to simmer a little. Then add ½ cup butter, 1 tablespoon sugar, and some salt, and cook an additional 10 minutes.

FARINA SOUP WITH WATER

Sprinkle ¼ cup farina into a saucepan with 2 cups cold water, and cook, stirring constantly, until it begins to simmer. Then add 6 tablespoons butter and some salt, and cook an additional 10 minutes.

SAGO SOUP WITH MILK

Sprinkle ¼ cup French sago into a saucepan with 3 cups milk. Add 6 tablespoons butter and some salt, and simmer ½ hour, stirring so it does not burn. (If it gets too thick, you may add some milk.)

> *[Sago is a starch extracted from the spongy center of the stem of the sago palm tree. It is used as a thickener in recipes, and although tapioca has a slightly different texture, it is an acceptable substitute—use ¼ cup tapioca pearls in this recipe.—Ed.]*

RICE SOUP WITH WATER

Following package directions, cook ¾ cup rice [in 1½ cups water]. Then push through a sieve or purée in a food processor. Add ½ cup butter with some salt and sugar, and cook 10 minutes. Then beat 3 egg yolks with 1 tablespoon sugar, and stir into the soup. (If it is too thick, you may add a little water.)

RICE SOUP WITH MILK

Following package directions, cook ½ cup rice [in 1 cup water]. Add 3 cups hot milk, ½ cup butter, and some salt and sugar, and cook a bit more, about 10 minutes.

POTATO SOUP WITH MILK

Blanch 2 pounds thinly sliced potatoes, and put in a saucepan with 4 cups milk. Add 1 large [sliced] onion, some salt and pepper, and ½ cup butter. Cook until soft, about 30 minutes.

FARFEL WITH MILK

Following package directions, cook 1 cup farfel in a saucepan with 3 cups milk. Add 4 tablespoons butter and some salt and sugar, and cook about 10 minutes.

[See note for Chickpea Soup with Farfel, page 30.—Ed.]

NOODLES WITH MILK

Bring 1 quart milk to the boil. Add thin noodles, some salt and sugar, and ½ cup butter, and cook about 10 minutes.

MILK SOUP WITH EGG DROPS

Beat together 2 egg yolks, some salt and sugar, and 2 tablespoons flour. Beat the 2 whites into a meringue (the Polish Jews call this "snow") and fold into the batter. Bring 1 quart milk to the boil, and add the batter to the milk, 1 teaspoon at a time. Add some salt and 4 tablespoons butter, and cook about 10 minutes.

BEET BROTH WITH MUSHROOMS (PORCINI)

In 2 quarts water, cook 2 ounces dried mushrooms, 2 parsley roots [parsnips can be substituted], 4 carrots, 1 onion, and 1 celery root for 1 hour. Strain, and add the juice of 2 lemons to the broth. Meanwhile, grate 4 pounds roasted red beets, add to the soup, and cook for about 10 minutes, making sure the liquid remains sufficient. Add some salt and sugar. Strain out the beets, and add 4 egg yolks beaten with ½ cup milk. Serve with dumplings filled with cooked mushrooms.

[The soup is delicious with or without the yolks, and it is also good to retain some or all of the grated beets. The easiest way to prepare the beets is to roast them whole in foil in a hot oven. They can then be easily peeled and grated. Although Lewando has no recipe for mushroom dumplings, the recipe for Rice Stuffed with Mushrooms (see page 130) will make the traditional uszki, or miniature mushroom dumplings, to use in this soup.—Ed.]

PICKLE SOUP

Cook 1 celery root, 1 parsley root [a parsnip can be substituted], and 2 carrots in 6 cups water for 1 hour. Then strain, and add 2 cups brine from sour pickles. Cut up 3 sour pickles, 4 potatoes, the cooked carrots, and 10 Marinated Mushrooms [see page 181], and add to the soup with ½ cup green peas. Sauté 1 tablespoon flour in ½ cup melted butter, add to the soup, and cook for about 15 or 20 minutes, until the potatoes are soft. Before serving, add ½ cup sour cream and some [chopped fresh] dill.

BEET SOUP WITH CABBAGE

Roast 2 pounds unpeeled beets, and finely shred 1 pound cabbage. Then grate 2 carrots, 1 parsley root [a parsnip can be substituted], and 1 celery root, and cook them with the cabbage in 2 quarts water for 1 hour, adding salt and lemon juice or sour salt to taste (you can also add 4 tart apples, peeled and grated). Then peel and grate the cooked beets, and add them to the pot. Melt

½ cup butter in a pan with 1 tablespoon flour. Stir into the soup, and cook for 15 minutes. Serve with 1 tablespoon sour cream in each dish. Eat this with mashed potatoes.

CANNED-TOMATO SOUP

Cook 1 celery root, 2 parsley roots [parsnips can be substituted], 3 onions, and 4 carrots in 2 quarts water for 1 hour. Strain the soup, add one 15-ounce can tomatoes, and cook ½ hour. Meanwhile, sauté 1 tablespoon flour in ½ cup melted butter. Add to the tomato soup, sprinkling in some salt. Following package directions, cook 1 cup rice separately. When serving, add a little rice, sour cream, and [chopped fresh] dill to each dish.

TOMATO SOUP WITH NOODLES

Cook 3 large sliced onions and one 15-ounce can tomatoes in 6 cups water. Add some salt and 1 tablespoon flour sautéed in ½ cup butter, and cook everything for 1 hour. Strain the soup, discard the onions, and gradually add 2 cups hot milk. When serving, add some fine noodles, a little sour cream, and a little [chopped fresh] dill to each dish. You have to cook the noodles separately, following package directions.

SAUERKRAUT SOUP WITH MUSHROOMS (KAPUŚNIAK)

Grate 1 celery root and 2 carrots. Add to them 3 cups (1½ pounds) sauerkraut and 1½ ounces dried mushrooms (borovkes) [porcini or cèpes], and cook in 2 quarts water for 1 hour. Meanwhile, sauté 1 large grated onion and 1 tablespoon flour in ½ cup melted butter, stir into the cooked soup, and cook about 10 minutes. To serve, add 1 tablespoon sour cream to each dish.

BEET SOUP

Roast 4 pounds beets, and peel and grate them. Cook 1½ ounces dried mush-rooms, 2 parsley roots [parsnips can be substituted], 1 celery root, 2 leeks, and 2 carrots in 2½ quarts water for 1 hour, then strain and add lemon juice or sour salt to the resulting soup (according to your taste). Sauté 1 tablespoon flour in ½ cup melted butter, and add to the soup along with some salt. Then, and only then, add the grated beets, bring to a simmer, and remove from the burner. When serving, add 1 tablespoon sweet cream and some sugar to each dish.

PRESERVED SORREL SOUP

Cook 1 celery root, 2 parsley roots [parsnips can be substituted], 3 carrots, and 3 onions in 2 quarts water for 1 hour. Strain the soup, add 2 cups pre-served sorrel, and cook ½ hour. Meanwhile, sauté 1 tablespoon flour in ½ cup melted butter, and add to the soup, along with salt to taste. When serving, add 1 tablespoon sour cream to each dish. Eat this with mashed potatoes or farina pancakes.

[Jars of preserved sorrel are sold in grocery stores in neighborhoods with a significant Russian or Polish population.—Ed.]

UKRAINIAN BORSCHT

Add one 15-ounce can tomatoes to 6 cups water, along with ½ pound cabbage cut into squares, 3 diced potatoes, and 1 tablespoon salt. Grate 1 celery root, 1 parsley root [a parsnip can be substituted], 2 red beets, and 2 carrots. Add them to the pot, and cook everything together for 1 hour. Then sauté 2 grated onions in 10 tablespoons (5 ounces) melted butter with 1 tablespoon flour, and add to the soup. Cook 20 minutes. When serving, add sour cream and [chopped fresh] dill and parsley to each dish. (In the summertime, make this borscht with 3 pounds fresh tomatoes instead of the 15-ounce can.)

CABBAGE AND APPLE BORSCHT

Finely shred 2 pounds cabbage (about 1 head), and grate 1 parsley root [a parsnip can be substituted], 2 carrots, 1 celery root, and 2 peeled tart apples. Add to cabbage, along with the juice of 1 lemon. Cook in 2 quarts water for 1 hour. Meanwhile, sauté 2 large grated onions in ¾ cup (6 ounces) melted butter with 1 tablespoon flour, and add to the soup. Sprinkle in salt and sugar to taste. Serve with 1 tablespoon sour cream in each dish.

BRAN BORSCHT

Pour 3 quarts boiling water onto 5 cups (1 pound) wheat bran in an earthenware pot, cover, leave to rest in a warm place for 48 hours, and then strain through a sieve. Take 1 quart of the liquid and add ½ pound shredded cabbage, 1 tablespoon flour sautéed in 4 tablespoons melted butter, ½ cup sour cream, and some salt and pepper, and cook for 20 minutes. Eat this with cooked potatoes. (Add a little more water to the remaining liquid and refrigerate it, so you can use it for a subsequent borscht.)

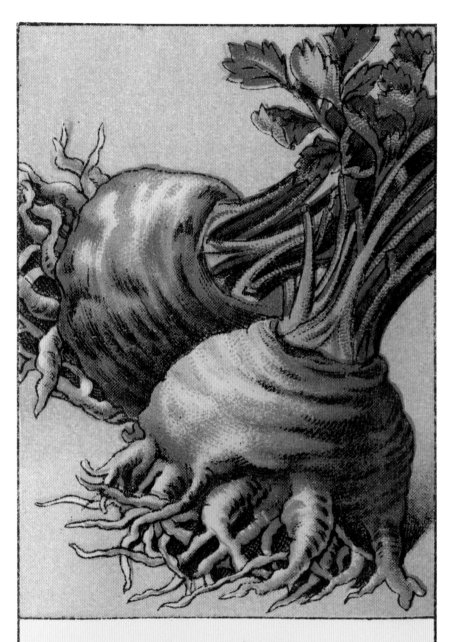

סעלערי
Celery

Cutlets

CHICKPEA CUTLETS

After soaking them overnight, cook 3 cups dried chickpeas until soft. Push them through a food mill, or purée in a food processor. Add 3 raw eggs, some salt, 4 tablespoons bread crumbs, and 3 tablespoons melted butter. Shape into cutlets, dip in bread crumbs, and fry in butter until brown. You may also serve some boiled, thinly sliced potatoes along with these.

CABBAGE CUTLETS

Shred 1 cabbage (about 2 pounds), boil in water for 20 minutes, squeeze dry, and push through a food mill or purée in a food processor. Add 3 raw eggs, 4 tablespoons bread crumbs, and some salt, and mix. Shape into cutlets, dip in bread crumbs mixed with 1 egg, and fry in butter until brown. Serve with stewed carrots.

NUT CUTLETS

Finely chop 1½ cups of the best walnuts. Then cook ¾ cup semolina in 1 quart milk until thick, about 10 to 15 minutes, stirring frequently. Allow it to cool, and push through a food mill. Then add the ground nuts to the semolina porridge, along with 3 tablespoons bread crumbs, 3 raw eggs, and 2 tablespoons melted butter. Mix well, and shape into cutlets. Dip in bread crumbs mixed with 1 egg, and fry in butter until brown. You can eat this with stewed carrots and green peas.

BEAN CUTLETS

After soaking them overnight, cook 1 cup dried beans until soft [or use 1 can of beans]. Thinly slice 2 large onions, sauté them in butter, and push them through a food mill along with the cooked beans. Add 4 tablespoons bread crumbs, 3 tablespoons melted butter, 3 raw eggs, and some salt. Mix well, and shape into small cutlets. Beat 1 egg, mix with 1 tablespoon bread crumbs, dip the cutlets in this, and fry in butter until brown. Serve with stewed cabbage.

[White beans, such as Great Northern, navy, and cannellini, work well for this recipe.—Ed.]

EGG CUTLETS

Hard-boil 6 eggs. Slice 2 large onions, and sauté in 2 tablespoons melted butter. Chop everything up together. Add 4 raw eggs, 3 tablespoons melted butter, 4 tablespoons bread crumbs, some salt, and some minced [fresh] parsley. Mix well, shape into cutlets, and fry in butter until brown. Serve with green peas.

BUCKWHEAT KASHA CUTLETS

Following package directions, cook 1 cup buckwheat groats. Soak 1 ounce dried mushrooms until soft, and sauté 2 minced onions in 2 tablespoons melted butter. Cut up the mushrooms and combine with onions and buckwheat groats. Beat in 3 raw eggs, 4 tablespoons bread crumbs, 2 tablespoons melted butter, and some salt. Mix well, and shape into little cutlets. Dip them in bread crumbs mixed with 1 egg, and fry in butter until brown. Serve with Mushroom Sauce.

[See note for Broad Noodles with Mushrooms, page 60.—Ed.]

CELERIAC CUTLETS

Cook 2 pounds celery roots (celeriac) with 3 leeks, drain, and purée in a food processor. Add 3 raw eggs, 2 tablespoons melted butter, 4 tablespoons bread crumbs, and some salt. Mix well, and shape into small cutlets. Dip in bread crumbs mixed with 1 egg, and fry in butter until brown. Serve with a side dish of carrots and beets.

SPINACH CUTLETS

Cook 2 pounds spinach, squeeze out the water, and push through a food mill or purée in a food processor. Add 2 tablespoons melted butter, 4 raw eggs, 5 tablespoons bread crumbs, and some salt, and mix well. Shape into small cutlets, dip them in an egg mixed with bread crumbs, and fry in butter until brown. You may serve these with a sour-cream sauce.

> *[This recipe is better with spinach chopped by hand. Form the mixture into cutlets of about ⅓ cup. The spinach-egg batter is very soft, and dipping and dredging is delicate work. Two pounds spinach will make a dozen 4-inch cutlets. It will take about 2 eggs and 2 tablespoons bread crumbs to make the batter sufficient for this recipe, plus an additional 2 tablespoons crumbs to coat the cutlets before cooking.—Ed.]*

CAULIFLOWER CUTLETS

Cook a cut-up large head of cauliflower in salted water, and push through a food mill or purée in a food processor. Add 2 tablespoons melted butter, 4 tablespoons bread crumbs, and 3 eggs. Mix well, and shape into cutlets. Mix 2 eggs with bread crumbs, dip the cutlets, and fry in butter until brown. Serve with stewed carrots.

YELLOW MUSHROOM *(LISITSHKES)* CUTLETS

Wash 1½ pounds yellow mushrooms [chanterelles or golden trumpets] in several changes of water, and scald them a few times in boiling water. Then cook, drain, and push through a food mill or purée in a food processor. Dice 1 onion, and sauté in 4 tablespoons melted butter. Add to the mushrooms, along with some [chopped fresh] dill, 5 tablespoons bread crumbs and some salt. Mix well, shape into cutlets, dip in an egg mixed with bread crumbs, and fry in butter until brown. Serve with new potatoes and steamed carrots.

> *[Other varieties of mushrooms may be used for the cutlets.—Ed.]*

POTATO CUTLETS STUFFED WITH MUSHROOMS

Cook and mash 2 pounds potatoes. Add 3 raw eggs, 1 tablespoon flour, 3 tablespoons bread crumbs, and some salt, and mix well. Meanwhile, cut up 2 ounces dried mushrooms that have been soaked in water till softened, 2 onions that have been fried in butter, 2 hard-boiled eggs, and some salt, and mix well. Shape cutlets with the potato mixture, fill with the mushroom mixture, and fry in butter. Serve with Mushroom Sauce [see page 127].

LIMA BEAN CUTLETS

Cook 1 cup lima beans, and push through a food mill or purée in a food processor. Add 2 tablespoons melted butter, 3 eggs, some salt, 3 tablespoons bread crumbs, and a little [chopped fresh] dill, and mix well. Shape small cutlets, mix an egg with some bread crumbs, dip the cutlets, and fry in butter. Serve with fried potatoes and Fresh Cucumber Salad [see page 17].

OAT CUTLETS

Boil 2 cups water, add 1 cup whole oats, 2 tablespoons butter, and some salt, and cook according to package directions. Chop 1 onion and a little [fresh] dill, and add 3 eggs and 1 cup bread crumbs. Mix well with the cooled oats, shape into cutlets, dip in bread crumbs mixed with 1 egg, and fry in butter. Serve with steamed cabbage.

פֿאַמידאָרן
Toma toes

Stewed Dishes

PRUNE *TSIMMES*

Cut 1 pound potatoes into thin slices. Remove the pits from 10 ounces of the best prunes. Lay layers of the potatoes and prunes in a baking pan, and pour on 1 cup water. Add ¾ cup sugar, and a roux made with 1 tablespoon flour, 1½ teaspoons butter, and a little salt. Bring to a boil, simmer uncovered for 20 minutes, place in baking dish, cover with water and bake, covered, 1 hour. Add 1 tablespoon sugar, caramelized, to the top.

STEWED ZUCCHINI WITH FRIED POTATOES

Peel 1 zucchini, and slice into thin rounds. Beat 2 eggs with 1 tablespoon flour. Dip the slices in this batter, sauté in butter, and then lay them in a baking pan. Add 4 tablespoons sour cream and some salt, and bake 15 minutes. Serve with fried potatoes sprinkled with [chopped fresh] dill.

> [The squashes available to Fania must have been larger and tougher than those currently available. Use a medium (8-ounce) zucchini, and skip the peeling.—Ed.]

STEWED CUCUMBERS

Peel 4 cucumbers, and cut into thick slices. Sprinkle with flour, and sauté in butter. Then lay them in a baking pan, and add salt, pepper, [chopped fresh] dill, and ½ cup sour cream mixed with 1 teaspoon flour, and bake 25 minutes.

CUCUMBERS STEWED WITH TOMATOES

Peel and thinly slice 3 green cucumbers, 1 pound firm tomatoes, and ½ pound onion, and sauté everything in 12 tablespoons (6 ounces) butter. Put the vegetables into a baking pan, sprinkle with salt, pour on ½ cup sour cream mixed with 1 tablespoon flour, and bake 20 minutes. Serve with fried potatoes.

SAUERKRAUT WITH PEAS

Cook 1 pound peas until soft, and strain. Cook 3 pounds sauerkraut separately, in its brine. Meanwhile, sauté 2 grated onions in 8 tablespoons butter with 1 tablespoon flour until brown. Add this to the sauerkraut, along with some salt and pepper, and bake 1 hour. Sauté 1 tablespoon bread crumbs in ½ cup butter. Pour this over the peas, and serve them alongside the stewed sauerkraut.

[Even though the sauerkraut is quite salty, some salt should be added to the buttered peas.—Ed.]

STUFFED CABBAGE

Cook 1 whole head cabbage and then separate the individual leaves. Cook 1 ounce dried mushrooms, 2 celery roots, and 2 leeks in water. Purée in a food mill or food processor. Add 1 cup cooked rice, ½ cup bread crumbs, and 3 eggs, and mix everything well. Then put a heaping tablespoon of filling into each cabbage leaf, and roll it up well so that the batter won't fall out. Pour 2 cups [one 15-ounce can] canned tomatoes into a baking pan, and add the cabbage rolls. Top with 2 large sliced apples, sprinkle with 5 tablespoons sugar, and dot with ½ cup butter. Cover tightly, and bake 1 hour. Then mix 1 tablespoon flour with 3 tablespoons water and 6 tablespoons sour cream. Pour this over the cabbage, cover tightly again, and bake 25 minutes. Eat this with mashed potatoes.

> [Cook the whole head of cabbage in a large pot of boiling salted water about 25 minutes, or until tender. Peel, trim, and chop the celery roots and leeks, and cook them and the mushrooms in enough of the leftover cabbage water to cover. Save the stock for making one of the soups (see the recipes for soups on pages 24 to 39).]

STEWED CABBAGE

Cut 1 head cabbage into quarters, cook in a little water, just to cover, until soft, and drain. To the liquid add 12 tablespoons (6 ounces) butter, 1 tablespoon flour, 1 teaspoon sugar, salt, pepper, and [chopped fresh] parsley, and cook 10 minutes. Then add the cabbage to the soup, along with 1 cup sour cream, and bake in the oven 20 minutes.

STEWED CABBAGE WITH POTATOES

Cut 1 large head cabbage into small pieces, and blanch in salted water. Strain out the water. Add ⅓ cup raisins, 1 pound sliced apples, and ½ cup sugar to 1 cup canned tomatoes, and pour everything onto the cabbage. Mix, and then cook 10 minutes. Meanwhile, melt ½ cup butter with 1 tablespoon flour. Add this to the cabbage, place in a baking pan, and bake in a hot oven 1 hour. Serve with mashed potatoes.

SAUERKRAUT STEWED WITH SOUR CREAM

Sauté 1 large diced onion in ½ cup butter. Rinse 2 pounds sauerkraut, strain in a colander, and place in a baking pan. Add the sautéed onion, 1 cup sour cream mixed with 1 tablespoon flour, and 3 tablespoons sugar, and bake ½ hour. Eat this with pease porridge.

> [Thinly sliced rather than diced onions harmonize better with the sauer-kraut. It is easier to mix the flour into the sour cream if it is sifted, but this is not necessary. Three tablespoons of sugar sounds like an outra-geous amount, but in fact it is just right. There is no pease porridge in the porridge chapter, but the peas in the recipe for Sauerkraut with Peas on page 49 should work here.—Ed.]

STEWED CABBAGE WITH RICE

Shred 1 large head cabbage, and massage with a little salt. Melt ½ cup butter in a pan, and sauté the cabbage. Grate 3 large onions, and sauté separately in ¼ cup butter. Mix everything together with 2 cups cooked rice. Add some salt and pepper. Grease a baking pan with 1 tablespoon butter, sprinkle with bread crumbs, pour in the mixture, add ¼ cup melted butter, and bake 25 minutes.

STEWED NEW POTATOES WITH SOUR CREAM

Dice 4 large onions, and sauté in ¼ cup butter. Melt ½ cup butter in a pan, and add 3 pounds thinly sliced new potatoes. Then mix the fried onions with the potatoes, add some salt and 1 cup green peas, cover tightly, and bake 1 hour. Now pour on 1 cup sour cream mixed with 1 tablespoon flour, add some [chopped fresh] dill, and steam, covered, 20 minutes.

STEWED POTATOES WITH TOMATOES

Sauté 3 large grated onions in 1 cup butter. Purée 1 pound tomatoes in a food mill or food processor. Add the tomatoes to the onions, and sauté in the pan

5 minutes, mixing so it does not burn. Slice 2 pounds potatoes, and put in a pan with some salt, 2 bay leaves, and the tomato sauce. Cover tightly, and bake in the oven long enough for the potatoes to become soft, about 45 minutes. Then add ½ cup sour cream and bake 10 more minutes.

NEW BABY CARROTS WITH FRESH BABY POTATOES

Cook 2 pounds new baby potatoes and 1 bunch new baby carrots in a pot with 3 cups water until they are halfway done. Pour out the water, add ¼ cup butter and a little salt, and place in oven, covered. When the vegetables become soft, pour on ¼ cup melted butter mixed with 2 tablespoons bread crumbs. Serve sprinkled with [chopped fresh] dill.

STEWED POTATOES STUFFED WITH MUSHROOMS

Hollow out 12 large potatoes (remove the insides). Soak 2 ounces dried mushrooms until soft. Meanwhile, sauté 2 large sliced onions in butter, and purée them with the mushrooms in a food mill or food processor. Add 4 tablespoons bread crumbs, ¼ cup butter, 2 eggs, and some salt. Mix well, and fill the hollowed-out potatoes. Slice 2 raw onions, and lay them in a stoneware pot with 2 tablespoons [melted] butter. Salt each potato, and brush with butter. Cover tightly, and bake 1 hour.

[Add about ½ cup water to the pan with the raw onions. Bake tightly covered for the first 45 minutes, and uncovered for the last 15.—Ed.]

STEWED POTATOES WITH SOUR CREAM

Thinly slice 3 large onions and 4 pounds potatoes, and sauté the onions in butter. Thinly slice 2 ounces soaked dried mushrooms, and mix with the fried onions. In a [buttered] baking dish, place a layer of potatoes, then some of the mushrooms and onions; dot with butter, and add another layer of potatoes, and then onions and mushrooms with butter, until everything is used up (you will have added ¾ cup [6 ounces] butter). Sprinkle with salt and a little pepper, and bake, covered, in a hot oven, so it will stew. When the potatoes are soft, in about 45 minutes, add 1 cup sour cream along with 1 tablespoon flour fried in 1 tablespoon butter. Bake in the oven 15 minutes more. Once done, eat immediately. It can be sprinkled with [chopped fresh] dill.

POTATOES STEWED IN SOUR CREAM

Thinly slice 4 pounds potatoes, and sprinkle with a little flour and salt. Melt ¾ cup butter in a pan, put in the potatoes, pour on ½ cup sour cream (mixed with 1 cup milk), and bake 1 hour. Serve sprinkled with [chopped fresh] dill and parsley.

STEWED TOMATOES

Slice 2 large onions, put them in a pan with ½ cup butter, and stew in the oven for 20 minutes. Cut 6 large tomatoes into small pieces, salt them, and add to the pan with the stewed onions. Cover, and bake in the oven for 10 minutes. Then beat 3 eggs, pour them over the tomatoes, and bake in the oven 5 minutes.

STEWED MUSHROOMS (CHANTERELLES)

Clean 2 pounds mushrooms, and blanch in hot water. Rinse them in cold water to remove all the grit and cook in 1 quart water for 10 minutes. After cooking, drain the mushrooms and add 1½ cups milk and 2 large onions that have been sautéed in ½ cup butter with 1 tablespoon flour. Add salt and pepper, and bake, covered, in a hot oven 1 hour. Then add 1 cup sour cream, and stew in the oven 1 more hour. Serve with new potatoes.

STEWED RICE WITH DUTCH CHEESE

Melt 1 cup butter in a pan. Sprinkle in 1½ cups rice, and sauté until golden brown. Pour the rice into a pot, and add 1 cup hot water; bring to the boil, and cook until soft. Grate 6 ounces Dutch cheese, add to the pot, mix well, and bake 30 minutes. Serve sprinkled with [chopped fresh] dill.

[Add 3 cups water to cook the rice. Gouda cheese works well for this recipe.—Ed.]

STEWED PEARS

Peel and core 2 pounds pears, place in a pot, and add the juice of 1 lemon, 1 cup sugar, and 1 envelope vanilla powder. Cover tightly and stew in the oven until brown. Then sauté 1 tablespoon flour in ½ cup butter, mix with ½ cup sour cream, pour over the pears, and return to the oven 20 minutes. Serve with Semolina Porridge [see page 86].

[Vanilla powder can be found in Russian delicatessens or online, or use 1 teaspoon vanilla extract instead.—Ed.]

STEWED ASPARAGUS

Cut off and discard the tough stems of 4 pounds thin asparagus. Put asparagus in a pot with 1 quart water, cook about 10 minutes, and then strain. Add ½ cup butter, ½ cup milk mixed with 1 tablespoon flour, and some salt, and mix everything together. Bake ½ hour. Beat 2 egg yolks with a little sugar, mix with 3 tablespoons sour cream, pour over the stewed asparagus, and serve.

[This recipe was written for white asparagus, which requires a longer cooking time and has tough, woody stems that would need to be discarded, thus requiring 4 pounds asparagus to get about 2 pounds edible tips. If green asparagus is used, only 2 pounds are necessary, even with the stem ends removed.—Ed.]

STEWED LENTILS

Pick over and cook 2 cups [1 pound] lentils [in water with salt] until soft. Meanwhile, grate 2 onions and sauté in ¾ cup [6 ounces] butter. Take ½ cup broth from the lentils, and add 1 tablespoon flour, ½ cup sour cream, and a little salt, pepper, and [chopped fresh] dill. Mix with the sautéed onions, pour this over the lentils in a pan, and bake, covered, 1 hour.

STEWED KOHLRABI

Cook 5 kohlrabies in boiling water until soft. Then take them out, peel, and cut into thin strips. Lay them in a pan, and add ½ cup butter, some salt, and ½ cup milk mixed with 1 teaspoon flour. Mix everything together, and bake ½ hour. Serve [sprinkled] with bread crumbs cooked in butter.

רויטע קרויט
Red Cabbage

Miscellaneous Dishes

IMITATION VEAL "MEATLOAF"

Combine 1 clove garlic, 2 bay leaves, 3 allspice berries, 2 onions diced and fried in butter, 1 small cooked celery root, 1 head cooked cabbage, and 1 bread roll soaked in milk. Purée everything in a food mill or food processor, and then add 5 raw eggs, 1 cup bread crumbs, 10 tablespoons melted butter, and some salt and pepper. Mix everything well, and form it into a meatloaf. Grease a pan with butter, and cover the bottom with 2 sliced onions and 3 sliced potatoes. Put in the meatloaf, and bake uncovered ½ hour. Then cover and bake 20 minutes. Serve with cranberry sauce.

STUFFED IMITATION KISHKE

Mash 1 pound cold cooked potatoes. Add 3 eggs, 2 tablespoons flour, 4 tablespoons bread crumbs, and some salt, and knead into a dough. Dust the counter with flour, and roll the dough into ¼-inch-thick sheet. Soak 2 ounces dried mushrooms, and purée in a food mill or food processor with onions that have been sautéed in butter. Mix this well with 1½ cups bread crumbs, 2 tablespoons flour, 1 cup melted butter, 2 eggs, some salt, [chopped fresh] dill, and a little [chopped fresh] parsley. Spread this over the dough, and roll it up like a kishke. Grease a small baking dish with butter. Line it with sliced potatoes and onions, and lay the kishke on top. Bake uncovered until it begins to brown, and then cover and continue baking until done, about 25 minutes.

IMITATION FISH MADE OF VEGETABLES

In a food mill or food processor, purée 1 head cooked cauliflower, 3 hard-boiled eggs, 3 onions that have been sautéed in butter, 2 raw onions, and 1 raw and 1 cooked celery root. Then add 1 cup bread crumbs, 1 torn-up slice bread soaked in milk, 10 tablespoons melted butter, 4 eggs, and some salt and pepper, and mix well. Shape the mixture into medium-size patties of fish, dip in bread crumbs, and sauté in butter. Then slice 3 onions and place in a baking pan with 6 tablespoons butter and the fish patties, and bake 25 minutes. Serve with horseradish sauce, or eat with plain horseradish.

IMITATION CAVIAR MADE OF SAGO

Cook 5 tablespoons French sago, strain, and squeeze over it the juice of 1 lemon. Meanwhile, grate 2 carrots and ¼ Spanish onion, and add some salt. Mix with the sago, and pour in ½ cup [olive] oil. Spread the caviar on buttered rolls, and serve.

[See note for Sago Soup, page 26.—Ed.]

JERUSALEM ARTICHOKES

Peel 2 pounds of Jerusalem artichokes, and cook in salted water, making sure they do not overcook. Mix 4 tablespoons melted butter with 1 tablespoon bread crumbs. Pour this over the artichokes, and serve with salad.

POTATO AND MUSHROOM ROAST

Thinly slice 2 large onions and 1 celery root, and sauté in ½ cup butter. Put in a roasting pan, and add 2 pounds sliced potatoes, 2 ounces dried mushrooms that have been soaked in water, 3 tablespoons butter, and some salt and pepper. Roast in the oven, covered, until the potatoes are soft. Then mix the broth from soaking the mushrooms with ½ cup sour cream, pour over the roast, and bake in the oven, uncovered, 20 minutes more.

PEARS WITH POTATOES

Peel 2 pounds large firm pears, cut them into quarters, place in a pot, and add 4 tablespoons sugar, ½ cup butter, some salt, [ground] allspice, a couple of bay leaves, the juice of ½ lemon, and 1 pound sliced potatoes. Cover, and put in the oven to stew for 30 to 40 minutes.

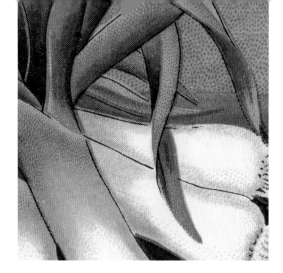

LEEKS WITH BUTTER

Cook 10 slender leeks in salted water, and drain. Melt ½ cup butter, add
2 tablespoons bread crumbs, and pour over the leeks.

NOODLES WITH NUTS

Following package directions, cook ½ pound thin noodles, and drain. Add
1 cup ground walnuts, 5 tablespoons sugar, and 6 tablespoons melted butter,
and mix well.

BROAD NOODLES WITH MUSHROOMS

Cook ¼ pound mushrooms, drain, and add 2 large sliced onions that have
been sautéed in butter; purée everything in a food mill or food processor with
some salt. Then cook ½ pound broad noodles, following package instructions, drain, and mix with the mushroom sauce. Add ½ cup melted butter
and mix well.

> [Cook the mushrooms in barely enough water to cover, and process them
> when they have absorbed the liquid. This recipe makes enough sauce to
> coat ½ pound noodles nicely but seems too sparse for a whole pound.—Ed.]

NOODLES WITH PRUNES

Soak 2 cups prunes, ¼ cup dried apples, and ½ cup sugar in 4 cups water, and then cook 1 hour [in the same water]. Cook the noodles separately, following package instructions. When serving, put some noodles in each dish and pour on some prunes.

BROAD NOODLES WITH SWISS CHEESE

Following package directions, cook 12 ounces broad noodles in salted water, and drain. Grate 6 ounces Swiss cheese, add some pepper, and mix with the noodles. Melt 12 tablespoons butter in a pan, mix with 3 tablespoons bread crumbs, and pour over the noodles. Sprinkle with [chopped fresh] dill and parsley.

BEANS WITH BUTTER

Cook for ½ hour in salted water 2 cups dried beans that have been soaked overnight, and drain. Melt ½ cup butter in a pan, mix with 2 tablespoons bread crumbs, and pour over the beans. Sprinkle with [chopped fresh] dill and parsley.

SAVOY CABBAGE WITH BUTTER

Cut 1 small head Savoy cabbage into quarters, and cook in salted water. Melt 12 tablespoons butter in a pan, mix with 3 tablespoons bread crumbs, and pour over the cabbage. Serve with potatoes fried in butter.

GREEN PEAS WITH TOASTED FARFEL

Mix 2 cups cooked toasted farfel with ½ cup cooked green peas. Add 12 tablespoons [melted] butter and some salt, and bake ½ hour. Serve with Mushroom Sauce [see page 127].

[See note for Chickpea Soup with Farfel, page 30.—Ed.]

RICE WITH APPLES

Following package directions, cook 1½ cups rice [in 3 cups water] until soft, and rinse in a colander with cold water. Add 2 grated apples, 1 cup raisins, ¼ teaspoon almond extract, a bit of cinnamon, 12 tablespoons butter, and 4 tablespoons sugar. Mix well, and bake 30 minutes. Serve with a plum sauce.

[Try substituting honey for butter for the New Year (or any occasion).—Ed.]

RICE WITH MUSHROOMS

Soak 4 ounces dried mushrooms in 2 cups water until soft. Drain, and purée in a food mill or food processor with 2 onions that have been fried in butter. Add salt and [chopped fresh] parsley and dill, and mix well. Meanwhile, following package directions, cook 1½ cups rice [in 3 cups water] until soft, mix with the puréed mushrooms, and add 12 tablespoons butter. Serve with a sauce made from the mushroom broth.

RICE WITH RAISINS

Following package directions, cook 1¼ cups rice [in 2½ cups water] until soft. Drain, and rinse with cold water. Add 1 cup raisins, ¼ cup chopped almonds, ½ cup [melted] butter, and 3 raw eggs. Mix well, and bake 30 minutes. Then put in porcelain cups, and pour cream or jam over them. You can also eat this cold.

RICE WITH FARMER CHEESE

Following package directions, cook 1¼ cups rice [in 2½ cups water] until soft. Mix with ½ cup [melted] butter and ½ pound [or one 7-ounce package] of the best farmer cheese and some salt. Bake 15 minutes.

RICE WITH STRAWBERRIES

Following package directions, cook 1¼ cups rice [in 2½ cups water] with some salt for 15 minutes, and drain. Meanwhile, grease an earthenware dish with butter. Put in the rice, add ½ cup [melted] butter, and bake, tightly covered, ½ hour. Serve with strawberries that have been cooked with sugar.

[One pint strawberries cooked with 2 tablespoons sugar makes a savory-sweet dish.—Ed.]

RICE WITH WHIPPED CREAM

Following package directions, cook 1¼ cups rice in 2½ cups milk. Add 6 tablespoons butter, 1 cup raisins, ¼ teaspoon almond extract, and 1 teaspoon vanilla extract, and mix everything well in a bowl. Whip ½ cup heavy cream with ½ teaspoon confectioners' sugar, and pour on top of the rice. You may also top this with various jams.

RICE WITH SWISS CHEESE

Following package directions, cook 1¼ cups rice [in 2½ cups water] until soft. Drain, and rinse with cold water. Grease a pan with butter, spread a third of the cooked rice in a thin layer on the bottom, and pour 3 tablespoons melted butter on it. Grate 6 ounces Swiss cheese, and scatter half over the rice. Spread on another layer of rice, pour on 3 more tablespoons melted butter, and cover with the remaining cheese. Top with the last of the rice, pour on another 3 tablespoons butter, and bake 1 hour. Serve with Mushroom Sauce [see page 127].

CREAMED GREEN PEAS

After soaking them overnight, cook ⅓ cup dried green peas until they are soft and only 2 tablespoons broth remain. Meanwhile, mix ½ cup milk, ½ teaspoon sugar, and 2 tablespoons butter. Pour over the peas, add a little salt, and bake 15 minutes.

CREAMED BEETS

Roast 2 pounds beets in their skins until soft, then peel and grate. Squeeze the juice from 1 lemon. Add 1 tablespoon sugar, 2 tablespoons sour cream, and some salt. Mix well with the beets, and heat until warm.

CREAMED SPINACH

Wash 2 pounds spinach well, cook briefly in a little water, drain, squeeze dry, and chop or put through a food mill. Put into a pan, add 2 tablespoons butter, some sugar and salt, and ½ cup sour cream, and bring to a simmer. Serve with fried bread rolls.

> [This flourless recipe makes a delicious creamed spinach for Passover (excluding the fried rolls). To make fried rolls, cut bread rolls in half and cook, cut side down, in butter.—Ed.]

CREAMED CARROTS

Cook 2 pounds carrots, and cut into little pieces. Mix 4 tablespoons butter, 1 tablespoon sugar, and some salt. Dissolve 1 tablespoon flour in 1 cup milk, and mix everything with the carrots. Pour into a dish, and bake 1 hour. In the summertime, add 1 cup green peas.

UKRAINIAN CHEESE *VARENIKES* [PIEROGI]

Make a soft dough from 2½ cups flour, 2 eggs, 1 tablespoon sour cream, and 1 tablespoon water. Roll out the dough, and cut out 3-inch square pieces as if for *kreplekh*. Press 1 pound farmer cheese (or two 7-ounce packages) through a sieve, and mix with 3 eggs, ½ cup butter, and some salt; fill and seal the dumplings. Bring 3 quarts salted water to the boil, add the *varenikes,* and cook 5 minutes. Then drain, put in a pan, add ½ cup butter and ½ cup sour cream, and heat 10 minutes. Serve with sugar and sour cream.

UKRAINIAN STRAWBERRY *VARENIKES* [PIEROGI]

Beat 3 eggs with 2 tablespoons water, and add as much flour as it will absorb [about 3 cups]. Knead the dough, and roll out into a thin sheet. Cut into 4-inch triangles, fill with strawberries mixed with sugar, and seal. Bring 4 quarts salted water to the boil, add the *varenikes,* and cook 5 minutes. Then drain, add 3 tablespoons melted butter, sprinkle with sugar, and pour on some sour cream.

CHERRY *VARENIKES*

Roll out a sheet of pasta dough, and cut into 4-inch squares. Meanwhile, remove the pits from 3 pounds cherries and mix with 1 tablespoon sugar. Put 4 cherries on each dough square, pinch to seal up like *kreplekh,* and cook in a large pot of boiling salted water 5 minutes. Then drain, add [melted] butter and sour cream to taste, and heat 10 minutes. Serve with sugar and sour cream.

[See Ukrainian Cheese Varenikes, above, to make pasta dough.—Ed.]

BAKED EGGS WITH PEPPER

Grease a small pan with butter, and sprinkle with bread crumbs. Break eggs into the pan, one at a time, and sprinkle each egg with pepper, salt, and finely diced onion. Put small pieces of butter between the eggs, and bake in the oven, about 15 minutes, or until yolks have set. Serve from the pan.

RICE DUMPLINGS

Following package directions, cook 1¼ cups rice [in 2½ cups water] until soft, and purée in a food mill or food processor with 2 onions that have been sautéed in butter. Then add some salt, [chopped fresh] parsley and dill, 5 tablespoons bread crumbs, 4 eggs, and ½ cup melted butter. Mix well, and shape into little dumplings. Roll them in bread crumbs mixed with an egg, and sauté in butter. Serve with Tomato Sauce [see page 126].

CHEESE DUMPLINGS WITH BREAD CRUMBS

Press 1 pound farmer cheese (or two 7-ounce packages) through a sieve. Add 1 cup bread crumbs, 3 tablespoons melted butter, 1 tablespoon sugar, 4 eggs, some salt, and a cup of raisins, and mix well. Shape into dumplings, and roll them in flour. Meanwhile, bring a large pot of water to the boil. Add some salt and the dumplings, without crowding, and cook 5 minutes. Remove with a slotted spoon, put in a pan, and pour on ½ cup melted butter mixed with 2 tablespoons bread crumbs. Bake in the oven 25 minutes. Serve with sugar and sour cream.

POTATO *ZRAZY* [STUFFED POTATO CAKES]

Mash 1 pound cold cooked potatoes, and mix with 3 eggs, 4 tablespoons butter, 1 tablespoon flour, and 3 tablespoons bread crumbs. Chop 2 hard-boiled eggs, and add 2 onions that have been thinly sliced and sautéed in butter, some salt, [chopped fresh] parsley and dill, 2 tablespoons bread crumbs, and 1 raw egg, and mix everything well. Fill the potato dough with this, make it into little *zrazy*, and cook in butter.

[In Polish cuisine, zrazy *refers both to filets of meat rolled around a veg-etable filling and to a potato dough rolled around a meat or vegetable filling. The latter is the type of* zrazy *prepared here. To form the* zrazy, *put a lemon-sized lump of potato dough in the palm of your hand, flat-ten it out, and fill with the egg filling. Fold the dough over to enclose the filling and form the dumpling into a flat diamond or lozenge shape. Cook the potato lozenges on both sides in butter.—Ed.]*

POTATO DUMPLINGS

Grate 4 pounds peeled potatoes on a coarse grater, wrap them in a towel, and squeeze out the moisture. Mix the potatoes with some flour and a little salt, and form into small dumplings. Meanwhile, bring 4 quarts salted water to the boil. Add the dumplings, and cook 10 minutes. Then drain the dump-lings and dress them with ½ cup butter with toasted bread crumbs. As soon as it is done, eat immediately.

POTATOES WITH EGGS

Cook 2 pounds potatoes, and allow to cool. When they are cold, remove the skins, cut into slices, and sprinkle with salt. Melt ½ cup butter in a pan, and coat the potatoes. Meanwhile, beat 5 eggs with ½ cup milk, 1 tablespoon flour, and some salt. Pour this over the potatoes, and bake 20 minutes.

[This is similar to a Spanish tortilla.—Ed.]

RICE WITH EGGS

Following package directions, cook 1½ cups rice [in 2½ cups salted water] until soft, and rinse in a colander with cold water. Put into a pan with ¾ cup [6 ounces] melted butter, and mix in 4 eggs, some salt, and [chopped fresh] dill and parsley, and bake 1 hour, stirring frequently.

SPINACH PÂTÉ

Wash and cook 1 pound spinach. Place in a colander, and squeeze out the water. Then add 3 onions fried in [olive] oil, 4 hard-boiled eggs, 2 apples, 4 tablespoons bread crumbs, some salt, and 5 tomatoes. Purée everything in a food mill or food processor. Stir in 2 raw eggs and ½ cup [olive] oil. Grease a pan with oil, put in the batter, cover tightly, and bake in a hot oven ½ hour. Then spread it onto a flat plate to cool. Serve spread on rolls or buns with butter.

BIGOS [POLISH HUNTER'S STEW]

Cook white cabbage in boiling water. Shred, add sliced fresh mushrooms, and squeeze in the juice of 1 lemon. Add ½ cup [melted] butter, 1 bunch fresh sliced carrots, and some salt, and bake 1 hour. When it is done, pour on ¼ cup [melted] butter mixed with 1 tablespoon flour. Serve with new potatoes.

> [A traditional bigos combines fresh cabbage and sauerkraut with several kinds of cured meat (bacon, sausage, salt pork, and so on). This simple recipe is more of a gesture in the direction of bigos than an attempt to reproduce the dish. Use 1½ pounds mixed wild mushrooms, and brown the vegetables for several minutes before setting the pot in the oven to stew. Season with pepper.—Ed.]

CAULIFLOWER WIENER SCHNITZEL

Chop 1 small piece cooked cauliflower, mix with 1 large egg, 1 tablespoon bread crumbs, and some salt, and beat well. Melt ¼ cup butter in a frying pan, add the batter, and cook on both sides [until it starts to brown]. Serve topped with a fried egg, and garnish with fried new potatoes and a gratin of carrots [see Creamed Carrots, page 64].

> [For "a small piece" of cauliflower, use about 4 ounces (½ cup chopped). One cooked cauliflower would be enough for about 8 schnitzels.—Ed.]

CARROT SCHNITZEL

Dice 1 cooked carrot. Mix with 1 large egg, 1 tablespoon bread crumbs, and some salt, and beat well. Melt ¼ cup butter in a frying pan, add the batter, and cook on both sides [until it starts to brown]. Serve topped with a fried egg, and garnish with fried new potatoes and a gratin of beets [see Creamed Beets, page 64].

GREEN PEA SCHNITZEL

Beat 1 large egg with 2 heaping tablespoons green peas and some salt. Melt ¼ cup butter in a frying pan, add the batter, and cook on both sides [until it starts to brown]. Serve topped with a fried egg, and garnish with stewed cabbage and fried new potatoes.

STUFFED TOMATOES

Hollow out 4 large firm tomatoes, and sprinkle the insides with salt. Sauté 1 grated onion in butter. Add ½ cup bread crumbs, 6 tablespoons melted butter, some salt, pepper, and [chopped fresh] dill and parsley, and beat everything together with 3 raw eggs. Fill the hollowed-out tomatoes with this mixture. Grease a baking dish with butter, add the tomatoes, and bake in a warm oven 20 minutes.

CARROT FRITTERS (LITTLE CARROT SCHNITZELS)

Cook 1 pound carrots, and purée in a food mill or food processor. Then beat 3 eggs, melt 2 tablespoons butter, add 2 tablespoons bread crumbs and some salt, and mix everything together. Drop the batter by the spoonful into a frying pan, like pancakes, and cook in butter [until it starts to brown]. You can also fry thin slices of cooked potatoes alongside.

BEEFSTEAK FROM FRESH MUSHROOMS

Cook 10 large mushrooms (without the stems) in boiling salted water. Take each pair of mushrooms, sprinkle with pepper, dip in beaten egg, dredge in bread crumbs, and sauté in butter like a beefsteak. Meanwhile, thinly slice 1 onion, sprinkle with pepper and salt, sauté in butter until brown, and serve over the steaks.

[This recipe is ideal for portobello or large cremini mushrooms. To form the steaks, take 2 mushroom caps, sprinkle the gills with salt and pepper, and press them, gill sides together, to make a round steak. Repeat with all the mushrooms. Then dip the double-top mushroom sandwiches in egg and dredge in bread crumbs, as described in the recipe.—Ed.]

CELERIAC SCHNITZEL

Chop 1 cooked medium-sized celery root [celeriac] into small pieces. Add 1 teaspoon bread crumbs and some salt, and mix with 1 large egg. Melt ¼ cup butter in a frying pan, add the batter, and cook on both sides [until it starts to brown]. Serve topped with 1 whole fried egg, and garnish with stewed cabbage and a gratin of carrots [see Creamed Carrots, page 64].

SAVOY CABBAGE SCHNITZEL

Cook 4 ounces (½ cup) finely chopped Savoy cabbage about 10 minutes, add 1 teaspoon bread crumbs and some salt, and beat together with 1 large egg. Melt ¼ cup butter in a frying pan, add the batter, and cook on both sides [until it starts to brown]. Serve topped with 1 whole fried egg, and garnish with spinach and fried new potatoes.

FRIED ZUCCHINI (GREEN SQUASH)

Peel 1 young small squash, and thinly slice. Sprinkle with salt, and sauté in butter until brown. Grease a baking pan with butter, and add the squash slices. Beat together a batter of 4 eggs, 1 teaspoon flour, and 3 tablespoons milk. Pour into the pan along with ½ cup melted butter, and bake 20 minutes.

> [The squashes available to Fania must have been larger and tougher than those currently familiar. Use a medium (8-ounce) zucchini, and skip the peeling.—Ed.]

FRIED MUSHROOMS (PORCINI)

Rinse porcini mushrooms in several changes of water, and cut into slices. Add salt, pepper, and thinly sliced onion, and sauté in butter, stirring so it does not burn, until soft. Then put into a pot, pour on sour cream, and bake, covered, ½ hour.

RASPBERRY MOUSSE

Beat 6 egg whites into a meringue, and gradually beat in 3 tablespoons powdered [confectioners'] sugar and ¾ cup melted raspberry jelly. Continue beating until everything is absorbed.

ROLLS WITH JAM, FRIED IN BUTTER

Cut French bread rolls into slices, and cut off the crusts. Spread jam or marmalade on half of the slices, and cover them with the remaining slices. Beat 2 eggs with 1 cup milk, dip the jam sandwiches in this, and cook in butter [until it starts to brown]. Serve sprinkled with sugar.

FRIED SUMMER SQUASH

Thinly slice 2 pounds squash; blanch in boiling water and salt. Beat 2 eggs with bread crumbs, dip the squash slices in this, and cook in butter [until it starts to brown]. Serve with a gratin of beets [see Creamed Beets, page 64].

SQUASH WITH BLACKBERRIES OR JAM

Put 3 pounds sliced winter squash in a baking pan with 3 tablespoons sugar, some salt, and ½ cup of butter, and bake 1 hour. Then add 1 spoonful milk mixed with 1 tablespoon flour, and bake 15 minutes. Serve topped with blackberries or jam.

STUFFED ZUCCHINI (GREEN SQUASH)

Peel 1 medium squash, cut off the top, hollow it out, and sprinkle with salt. Take 2 hard-boiled eggs, 2 onions fried in butter, some salt, [chopped fresh] parsley and dill, 3 tablespoons bread crumbs, and 1 pound cooked mushrooms, and purée in a food mill or food processor. Following package directions, cook 1 cup rice [in 2 cups salted water] separately. Mix the vegetable batter with the rice, adding 2 raw eggs and ½ cup melted butter. Fill the squash with this, replace the top, and tie with a little string. Put in a baking pan, add butter, and bake.

> *[This recipe seems to be for globe zucchini. If using long zucchini, cut them lengthwise rather than cutting off the tops. In either case, it is not necessary to peel the squash. Though the instructions are for 1 squash, this amount of filling will fill 8 medium zucchini of either the long or the globe variety. Use kitchen twine to tie the squashes together for baking, or skip this step and bake them untied. Cover the squash for the first 20 minutes of baking. They will be done in 30 to 40 minutes, depending on their size and age.—Ed.]*

ASPARAGUS

Peel 1 pound asparagus, tie them together with string, and cook in salted water until soft. Then take them out, place on a dish, and dress with bread crumbs cooked in ¾ cup melted butter.

> *[Untie the asparagus before serving, or cook without tying them up.—Ed.]*

GIANT LIMA BEANS WITH LEMON SAUCE

Cook 1 pound giant lima beans (gigantes) until soft. Meanwhile, cook 1 tablespoon flour in ½ cup butter. Add ½ cup sour cream, some salt, 1 teaspoon sugar, and the juice of 1 lemon. Mix everything together, and pour over the beans. Bake 20 minutes.

עפינאד
Spinage

Blintzes (Stuffed Crepes)

BLINTZES FILLED WITH SPINACH

Wash and cook 1 pound spinach, and drain well. Add 2 hard-boiled eggs and 1 large onion that has been sautéed in butter, and purée everything in a food mill or food processor. Add 2 tablespoons bread crumbs, some salt, 1 raw egg, and 2 tablespoons [melted] butter. Spread a thin layer of the mixture onto the crepes, and cook in butter until brown.

[For crepes, see Cheese Blintzes, below.—Ed.]

BLINTZES FILLED WITH ALMONDS

Mix ¼ pound ground sweet almonds and ¼ teaspoon almond extract with 4 egg yolks and 2 tablespoons sugar. Beat the 4 egg whites into a meringue, and gently fold into the mixture. Fill crepes, and cook in butter until brown.

[For crepes, see the following recipe.—Ed.]

CHEESE BLINTZES

Beat 4 egg yolks with a little sugar and salt, adding 1 envelope vanilla powder [or 1 teaspoon vanilla extract]. Then add ½ cup milk and 2 cups of the best flour, and beat well. Gently fold into a meringue whipped from the 4 egg whites. Make the blintz crepes from this batter. Meanwhile, mix 1 pound farmer cheese with ¼ pound butter and 2 eggs, and put mixture through a sieve. Add 1 tablespoon sugar and ¾ cup raisins, and mix. Fill the crepes, and cook in butter until brown. Serve with sugar and sour cream.

RHUBARB BLINTZES

Wash 1 pound rhubarb, and cook with 1 cup sugar until it becomes thick, then purée with ½ envelope vanilla powder [or ½ teaspoon vanilla extract]. Fill crepes, and cook in butter until brown. Serve with sour cream and sugar.

[For crepes, see Cheese Blintzes, above.—Ed.]

BLINTZES FILLED WITH MUSHROOMS

Sauté 1 cup fresh mushrooms in oil until lightly browned. Add 3 onions fried in butter, a little [chopped fresh] dill and parsley, 2 hard-boiled eggs, ½ head Savoy cabbage, salt, and pepper, and purée everything well. Add 2 raw eggs, 3 tablespoons bread crumbs, ½ cup butter, and mix well. Fill the crepes, roll in bread crumbs, and cook in butter until brown.

[For crepes, see Cheese Blintzes, opposite.—Ed.]

BLINTZES FILLED WITH APPLES

Grate 2 pounds apples, add sugar to taste, and mix well. Fill the crepes, roll them up, and cook in butter. Serve with sugar and sour cream.

[For crepes, see Cheese Blintzes, opposite.—Ed.]

צ י ב ע ל ע
Onion

Omelets

ROLLED SPINACH OMELET

Wash and cook 1 pound spinach, drain, and chop. Add 4 tablespoons bread crumbs, some salt, ½ cup ground walnuts, 1 grated apple, 1 tablespoon butter, and 2 eggs, and mix well. Melt 2 tablespoons butter in a pan, pour in the mixture, and cook gently for a few minutes (this filling is enough for 4 omelets). Beat an egg yolk with some sugar, stir in 1 tablespoon milk and 1 teaspoon flour, and fold gently into a meringue beaten from the egg white. Melt 2 tablespoons butter in a pan, pour in the batter, and cook gently on both sides [until it starts to brown]. Then spread on [a quarter of] the spinach filling, roll it up, and cook for a few more minutes. Serve with a fruit sauce or jam. To make 4 omelets, you need to use 4 eggs.

TOMATO OMELET

Put 4 ripe tomatoes through a food mill (or peel, seed, and chop). Add 4 beaten eggs, ¼ cup milk, 1 tablespoon flour, and some salt and pepper, and mix well. Then melt 6 tablespoons butter in a pan. When the butter starts to sizzle, pour in the tomato mixture, and cook until brown.

CHEESE OMELET

In a bowl, mix 3 tablespoons bread crumbs with 1 cup hot scalded milk, cover, and let stand until the milk is absorbed. Then add 2 tablespoons [melted] butter, ½ pound grated cheese, and 4 beaten egg yolks. Whip the 4 whites into a meringue, and fold into the cheese mixture. Melt 6 tablespoons butter in a pan, and when the butter sizzles, pour in the mixture and cook on both sides until brown. This batter is enough for 3 omelets.

EGG AND JAM OMELET

Beat 3 eggs, and stir in 3 tablespoons milk and ½ teaspoon sugar. Meanwhile, melt 4 tablespoons butter in a pan, pour in the mixture, and when it is halfway done [about 5 minutes], add any kind of jam. Let it cook [about 5 minutes] more, and serve.

MUSHROOM OMELET

Stew 1 pound sliced mushrooms and 1 sliced onion in 4 tablespoons butter with some pepper and salt until soft. Beat 4 eggs, and add to the mixture. Then melt 2 tablespoons butter in a pan, add a quarter of the batter, and cook on both sides. Cook the remaining batter, to make 4 omelets. Serve with new potatoes sprinkled with [chopped fresh] dill.

DUTCH CHEESE OMELET

Pour 1 cup hot milk over 3 tablespoons bread crumbs, and allow to rest, covered, so that the crumbs can soak up the milk. Then add 4 tablespoons [melted] butter, ½ pound grated Dutch cheese, 4 well-beaten egg yolks, and some salt and pepper, and mix well. Beat the whites into a meringue, and gently fold into the mixture. Grease a pan with butter, pour in the batter, and bake in a hot oven until brown.

SWISS CHEESE OMELET

Grate ½ pound Swiss cheese. Add a little [chopped fresh] parsley, 2 thinly sliced leeks, 1 tablespoon bread crumbs, some salt and pepper, and 2 tablespoons melted butter. Add to this mixture 4 eggs and 1 teaspoon milk. Melt 2 tablespoons butter in a pan, add the batter, cook until brown, and serve at once.

SOUFFLÉ OMELET

Beat 6 egg yolks with 1 cup sugar until the mixture is pale. Add the juice and grated zest of 1 lemon and 3 tablespoons flour, and mix well. Beat the 6 egg whites into a meringue, and gently fold into the mixture. Grease a pan with butter, pour in the batter, and bake in a warm oven until brown.

ASPARAGUS OMELET

Cut the ends off 1 pound asparagus, and cook until tender in salted water. Cut into small pieces, and mix with 3 eggs. Add salt and a little [chopped fresh] dill and parsley. Melt 2 tablespoons butter in a pan, pour in the batter, and cook on both sides until brown.

SPINACH OMELET

Cook 1 pound spinach, drain well, and chop. Add salt, 2 tablespoons milk, 2 tablespoons bread crumbs, and 5 eggs, and beat everything together well. Melt 1 tablespoon butter in a pan, pour in a quarter of the batter, and cook on both sides. Repeat with remaining batter to make 4 omelets.

SPANISH ONION OMELET

Slice 2 large Spanish onions, and sauté in 4 tablespoons butter until soft. Beat 4 egg yolks, 1 tablespoon milk, 1 teaspoon flour, and some salt, and mix with a meringue beaten from the 4 egg whites. Pour this over the onions, and cook on both sides until brown. Serve sprinkled with [chopped fresh] dill.

קרוטשקע (ברוקװע)

Turnip

Porridges

MASHED POTATOES

Boil 4 pounds potatoes. Beat them well with a wooden spoon, and press through a sieve. Add 6 tablespoons butter and 1 cup hot milk. Mix well, and bake in a hot oven 10 minutes.

[This recipe may be reduced by half. Boil the potatoes in liberally salted water until tender, which will depend on the size of potatoes. Push them through a potato ricer, or mash with a masher or a fork.—Ed.]

RICE PORRIDGE

Pour 1¼ cups rice into a pot with 3 quarts boiling water, and cook until soft. Drain the rice, and rinse with cold water. Put the rice back in the pot, and add 6 tablespoons butter and some salt. Cover tightly, and bake 1 hour.

SEMOLINA PORRIDGE

Cook 2 cups semolina in 5 cups milk until it becomes a porridge. Meanwhile, slice ⅓ cup almonds into thin slivers, and add 1 teaspoon almond extract. Add 1¼ cups sugar, 1 cup raisins, 1 vanilla bean [or 1 teaspoon vanilla extract], and a bit of candied orange peel cut into small pieces. Mix everything with the cooked porridge. Grease a stoneware pot with butter, pour in the mixture, and sprinkle the top thickly with bread crumbs. Bake 1 hour. Remove vanilla bean [if using] before serving. This can be eaten cold or hot.

KRAKÓW KASHA (FINE SEMOLINA PORRIDGE) WITH SWISS CHEESE

Sauté 3 diced Spanish onions in 4 tablespoons butter. Add ½ pound grated Swiss cheese, and mix with Kraków Kasha (see the recipe opposite). Bake 15 minutes.

KRAKÓW KASHA (FINE SEMOLINA PORRIDGE)

Beat 3 raw eggs into 1 pound (1½ cups) fine semolina. Spread the semolina on a baking sheet, and bake until dry, stirring a few times so it toasts evenly. Meanwhile, heat 3 cups milk with 1 teaspoon salt. Sprinkle in the toasted semolina, add 7 tablespoons butter, cover tightly, and bake 1 hour. Eat this with honey.

BARLEY PORRIDGE

Cook 1 cup pearl barley in 2 cups milk until soft [about 40 minutes]. Then add some salt and 7 tablespoons butter. Cook about 10 more minutes.

BARLEY PORRIDGE WITH FARMER CHEESE

Cook ¾ cup pearl barley in 2 cups milk until soft [about 40 minutes]. Mix with 1 pound farmer cheese, ½ cup sour cream, some salt, and 6 tablespoons [melted] butter. Grease a stoneware pot with butter, and add the batter. Bake 15 minutes.

TOASTED FARFEL PORRIDGE

Make a firm dough with 4 cups flour and 4 eggs. Knead well, and shape into small pieces of farfel. Scatter the farfel on a baking sheet, and heat in the oven to dry, stirring often, until it becomes brown; then cook like all porridges.

[Add ½ teaspoon salt to the egg dough for the farfel. The dough will be quite firm. Chop the dough into lumps about the size of rice or barley grains. It will take about 25 minutes to brown in an oven heated to 350°F. In this chapter, some porridges are cooked in milk, some in water, some boiled, and some baked, so "cook like all porridges" is ambiguous. The toasted farfel can be cooked in boiling salted water for ½ hour and then dressed with butter and milk. Chopping would have been the method for making dough into farfel in Fania's Vilna. In other parts of the Yiddish *world, traditional methods of farfel preparation included cutting, pluck-ing, and grating the dough. See Marvin I. Herzog "The Yiddish Lan-guage in Northern Poland: Its Geography and History," in* International Journal of American Linguistics *31:2 (April 1965).—Ed.]*

BUCKWHEAT KASHA *(TATRKE)*

Pick over 1 pound buckwheat groats to remove all stones. Scatter on a baking sheet, and place in a hot oven to dry, stirring often, until toasted. Bring 2 cups water to the boil, and stir in the hot groats. Add 4 tablespoons butter and some salt, and bake, tightly covered, 1 hour, making sure it does not become too dry. When serving, add 1 pat of butter to each portion. You can also eat this with milk.

MILLET PORRIDGE

Soak 1 pound millet groats overnight in cold water. Drain, and put the groats in a pot with 2 cups hot milk, some salt, and ½ cup butter. Cover tightly, and bake 1½ hours, stirring frequently so it does not burn. Serve with butter or milk.

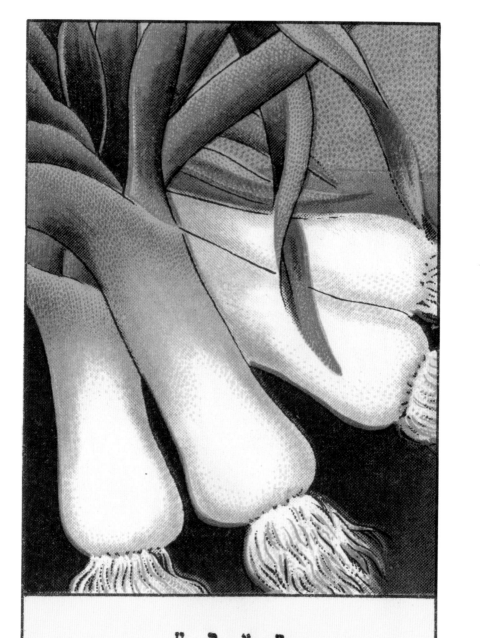

פְּרָ֫ר
Leek

Frittatas

RICE FRITTATA

Mix ½ cup cooked rice with ½ cup milk and 3 beaten eggs. Add some salt, and beat well. Melt 5 tablespoons butter in an oven-proof skillet, pour in the batter, and cook like a frittata.

[We take "cook like a frittata" to mean cooking the egg mixture on stovetop for a minute or two, until egg at the edges of the pan begins to set. Then put pan in oven and bake at 400°F, until eggs are set.—Ed.]

LEEK FRITTATA

Slice 5 leeks, and sauté in 6 tablespoons butter. Then beat 3 eggs with some salt, pour over the leeks, and cook like a frittata.

[This works best if the leeks are sliced very thin and cooked over low heat for 20 minutes. Fania's leeks must have been smaller than those available in farmers' markets today. Two large leeks will work well with 3 eggs.—Ed.]

FRIED POTATO FRITTATA

Thinly slice 5 cooked potatoes, sprinkle with salt and pepper, and sauté in butter until brown. Then pour in 2 beaten eggs, and cook until it becomes a frittata. Serve sprinkled with [chopped fresh] dill.

FRIED CAULIFLOWER FRITTATA

Cook 1 small head cauliflower in salted water. Break into pieces, and sauté in a pan with butter. Meanwhile, beat 3 eggs, add some salt, and pour over the cauliflower. Cook until it becomes a frittata.

TOMATO FRITTATA

Thinly slice 1 large tomato, sprinkle with pepper and salt, and mix with 2 beaten eggs. Meanwhile, melt 4 tablespoons butter in a pan. When the butter foams, add the eggs and tomato, and cook like a frittata.

קאלאפיער

Cauli flower

Kugels with Cholents

CAULIFLOWER AND CARROT KUGEL

Purée 1 small cooked cauliflower, and add ½ cup bread crumbs, ¾ cup raisins, 1 Antonovka apple cut into small pieces, 2 tablespoons sliced almonds, ¼ teaspoon almond extract, 2 tablespoons chopped candied orange peel, 3 tablespoons sugar, 5 tablespoons flour, 6 ounces (¾ cup) [melted] butter, 2 eggs, and some salt. Mix everything together well. Meanwhile, cook 4 pounds carrots, slice into little pieces, and lay half of them in a baking dish. Spread the kugel batter over them, and top with remaining carrots. Dot with ½ cup butter, 3 tablespoons sugar, and some salt, and pour on 1 cup milk mixed with 1 tablespoon flour. Cover tightly, and bake 1 hour.

[You can substitute for the Antonovka apple any tart, crisp variety, such as Cortland, Jonathan, or Winesap. If the full quantity is made, a large lasagna pan (11 by 17) will be needed to bake this.—Ed.]

NOODLE KUGEL

Make noodles with 2 eggs, cook them, and drain them. Add ½ cup [melted] butter, ¾ cup raisins, a little cinnamon, ½ teaspoon almond extract, 3 tablespoons sugar, the juice of ½ lemon, and 2 eggs. Mix well, and pour into a kugel pan [8-by-8 square pan]. Fill a larger baking dish with water, and place the kugel pan in the water bath. Bake until brown. (You can also include this in a *milkhik* cholent.)

[See recipe for Potato Kreplekh, page 131, to make the noodle dough. Or use one 10-ounce package of medium noodles, prepared according to package directions.—Ed.]

RICE KUGEL

Following package directions, cook 1¼ cups rice [in 2½ cups water] until soft, and add ½ cup plus 1 tablespoon [melted] butter, 4 tablespoons sugar, 1 large grated apple, ¾ cup raisins, ½ cup candied orange peel, ½ teaspoon almond extract, 2 eggs, and some salt. Mix well, and pour into a kugel pan [small loaf pan]. Fill a larger baking dish with water, and place the kugel pan in the water bath. Bake until brown. (You can also include this in a cholent.)

NOODLE KUGEL WITH NUTS

Make noodles from 2 eggs, cook them, and drain. Mix 4 tablespoons sugar, 1 cup ground walnuts, ½ cup plus 1 tablespoon [melted] butter, 4 ounces chopped figs, the juice of 1 lemon, grated zest of ½ lemon, and 2 eggs. Grease a kugel pan with butter, sprinkle with bread crumbs, and add the batter. Fill a larger baking dish with water, and place the kugel pan in the water bath. Bake until brown. (You can also include this in a cholent.)

[See recipe for Potato Kreplekh, page 131, to make the noodle dough. Or use one 10-ounce package of medium noodles, prepared according to package directions.—Ed.]

CREPE KUGEL WITH JAM

Make 6 small blintz crepes. Take 2 sliced apples and ¾ cup raisins, 2 tablespoons sliced almonds, ½ teaspoon almond extract, 1 cup chopped candied orange peel, ½ cup bread crumbs, 3 tablespoons jam (any kind), 7 tablespoons [melted] butter, and 2 tablespoons sugar, and mix well. Grease a kugel pan with butter, and sprinkle with bread crumbs. Put in 1 blintz crepe, spread with some of the jam mixture, and then add a second, and so on, until all have been used. Fill a larger baking dish with water, and place the kugel pan in the water bath. Bake until brown. (You can also include this in a cholent.)

[For crepes, see Cheese Blintzes, page 76.—Ed.]

CHALLAH KUGEL

Soak 2 slices of challah in milk. Mix with 2 tablespoons flour, ¾ cup raisins, 24 ground almonds, ½ teaspoon almond extract, the juice of 1 lemon, the zest of ½ lemon, 3 tablespoons sugar, 2 eggs, and ½ cup plus 1 tablespoon melted butter. Grease a kugel pan with butter, and add [a thin layer of] honey. Add the kugel mixture. Fill a larger baking dish with water, and place the kugel pan in the water bath. Bake 3 to 4 hours. (You can also include this in a cholent.)

BREAD CRUMB KUGEL

Mix 1 cup fine bread crumbs with 3 tablespoons flour, 3 tablespoons sugar, ¾ cup raisins, ½ teaspoon almond extract, 2 eggs, 1 sliced apple, and ½ cup plus 1 tablespoon [melted] butter. Grease a kugel pan with butter, sprinkle with bread crumbs, and add the batter. Fill a larger baking dish with water, and place the kugel pan in the water bath. Bake until brown. (You can also include this in a cholent.)

TOASTED KUGEL

Mix 1 cup bread crumbs with 3 tablespoons flour, ¾ cup raisins, 3 tablespoons sugar, a little cinnamon, the grated zest of 1 lemon, 2 tablespoons sliced almonds, 1 sliced apple, 1 tablespoon semolina, ½ cup plus 1 tablespoon [melted] butter, and 1 cup boiling water. Then beat in 2 eggs. Grease a kugel pan with butter, sprinkle with bread crumbs, and add the batter. Fill a larger baking dish with water, and place the kugel pan in the water bath. Bake until brown. (You can also include this in a cholent.)

MILKHIK CHOLENT WITH NEW POTATOES

In a cast-iron pot put 4 pounds halved potatoes, 2 sliced onions, 1 pound sliced carrots, 1 head cabbage cut into 6 pieces, 1 cup pearl barley, some salt, and 1 cup [melted] butter. Add enough water to cover mixture. Into this pot, put any kind of kugel (according to your taste), wrap in parchment paper, and tie with string. Cover pot tightly, and bake about 6 hours.

CHOLENT WITH BEANS, MUSHROOMS, AND POTATOES

In a cast-iron pot put 4 pounds halved potatoes, 2 sliced onions, 2 ounces dried mushrooms [that have been soaked until soft], chopped, 2 cups large lima beans that have been soaked overnight, some salt, and 1 cup [melted] butter. Add enough water to cover mixture. Into this pot, put any kind of kugel (according to your taste), wrap in parchment paper, and tie with string. Cover pot tightly, and bake about 6 hours.

PRUNE AND APPLE CHOLENT WITH POTATOES

In a cast-iron pot put 1 pound prunes (without the pits), 4 pounds halved potatoes, ¾ cup dried apples [that have been soaked until soft], some salt, 4 tablespoons sugar, and ½ cup plus 2 tablespoons [melted] butter. Add enough water to cover mixture. Into this pot, put any kind of kugel (according to your taste), wrap in parchment paper, and tie with string. Cover pot tightly, and bake about 6 hours.

קירבעס
Melon

Puddings

SPINACH PUDDING

Wash and cook 1 pound spinach, place in a colander, and squeeze out the water. Purée in a food mill or food processor. Add 3 grated apples, ½ teaspoon almond extract, 2 tablespoons ground almonds, ¾ cup raisins, 3 tablespoons sugar, and 6 egg yolks, and mix everything well. Beat the 6 egg whites into a meringue, and fold into the batter. Then grease a pan with butter, sprinkle with a thick layer of bread crumbs, pour in the batter, and bake in a hot oven 1 hour.

[Spinach-based desserts are a surprise to contemporary cooks, but according to Lynne Rossetto Kasper in The Splendid Table *(New York: William Morrow, 1992), they are found in recipes from northern Italy, France, and England in the eighteenth and nineteenth centuries, and pastries made with spinach remain popular in Emilia-Romagna to this day.—Ed.]*

BREAD CRUMB PUDDING

Beat 2 tablespoons butter with 2 tablespoons sugar until mixture is pale, and add the grated zest of 1 lemon. Bring 1½ cups milk to the boil, whisk it into the mixture, and allow to cool. Then add 4 eggs and 4 tablespoons bread crumbs, and continue to mix. Generously grease a stoneware dish with butter, and coat with bread crumbs. Add the batter, and bake 20 minutes.

APPLE CHARLOTTE WITH WHOLE-WHEAT BREAD CRUMBS

Thinly slice 1 large loaf of whole-wheat bread, and dry the slices in the oven. Take the dried slices of bread (rusks) and grind them in a food mill or food processor. Slice 2 pounds peeled apples into small pieces, and add 1 cup sugar, ½ teaspoon almond extract, ¾ cup raisins, some diced candied orange peel, ¾ cup butter, 1 envelope vanilla powder [or 1 teaspoon vanilla extract], 6 egg [yolks], and 1 cup [of the] ground whole-wheat bread crumbs, and mix well. Beat the 6 egg whites into a meringue, and gently fold into the batter. Grease a stoneware pan with butter, sprinkle with bread crumbs, pour in the batter, and bake in a warm oven 1 hour. Top with whipped cream.

[It is not clear why a whole loaf of bread crumbs is needed for a recipe that will use only 1 cup (4 ounces), plus those needed to coat the pan.—Ed.]

APPLE PUDDING WITH RICE

Following package directions, cook 1 cup rice [in 2 cups water] until soft, and rinse in cold water. Then add ¾ cup sugar, ¾ cup raisins, 1 envelope vanilla powder [or 1 teaspoon vanilla extract], 3 thinly sliced large apples, 6 egg yolks, and ¾ cup [6 ounces] [melted] butter, and mix everything well. Beat the 6 egg whites into a meringue, gently fold into the batter, and pour into a stoneware baking pan that has been buttered and lined with bread crumbs. Bake 1 hour.

SEMOLINA PUDDING

Stir 1 cup semolina into 4 cups simmering milk. Continue stirring and cooking until it becomes a thick porridge. Pour porridge into a bowl with ½ cup [melted] butter, ¾ cup raisins, ½ cup sugar, and 1 teaspoon almond extract. Mix everything together, then mix in 6 egg yolks and 1 envelope vanilla powder [or 1 teaspoon vanilla extract]. Whip the 6 egg whites into a meringue and gently fold into the batter. Pour into a baking pan that has been buttered and lined with bread crumbs, and bake in a warm oven ½ hour. Serve with fruit syrup or Cream Sauce [see page 127].

APPLE PUDDING

Take 1 pound French bread rolls [about 6 rolls or 2 baguettes], cut off the crusts, soak bread in milk, then squeeze out. Meanwhile, cut 1 pound apples into slices, and grind 3 tablespoons almonds. Add 1 envelope vanilla powder [or 1 teaspoon vanilla extract], ¾ cup raisins, and ½ cup [melted] butter, and mix everything together. Beat 3 egg yolks with ½ cup sugar until mixture is pale. Beat the whites into a meringue, and fold gently into the batter. Pour into a stoneware baking pan that has been buttered and lined with bread crumbs. Bake until brown.

PUDDING WITH BLINTZ WRAPPERS LAYERED WITH CHEESE

Press 1 pound (2 packages) farmer cheese through a sieve. Add 3 egg yolks beaten with ½ cup sugar, ¾ cup raisins, 2 tablespoons sour cream, 1 envelope vanilla powder [or 1 teaspoon vanilla extract], and ¾ cup [melted] butter, and mix everything well. Make 12 crepes for blintzes [see Cheese Blintzes, page 76], grease a baking pan with butter, and sprinkle with bread crumbs. Line the pan with a third of the crepes, spread half the filling on top, and repeat with another layer of crepes, and another layer of cheese filling, ending with a layer of crepes on top. Dot the top with 3 tablespoons butter, and bake until done, about 30 minutes.

FRESH MUSHROOM PUDDING (CHANTERELLES)

Wash 2 pounds chanterelles in several changes of water. Cook in salted water until soft, and drain. Meanwhile, cut 1 onion into small pieces, and sauté in 6 tablespoons butter. Purée everything in a food mill or food processor. Add 4 tablespoons bread crumbs, 4 egg yolks, ½ cup [melted] butter, and some pepper and salt, and mix well. Then make a meringue from the 4 egg whites, and fold gently into the batter. Pour into a baking pan that has been buttered and lined with bread crumbs. Bake 25 minutes.

MILKHIK APPLE PUDDING

Soak 3 rolls in milk, squeeze them out, and add 2 pounds sliced tart apples, 1 cup sugar, ½ cup butter, 1 envelope vanilla powder [or 1 teaspoon vanilla extract], and 5 egg yolks, and mix well. Beat the 5 egg whites into a meringue, and fold gently into the batter. Pour into a stoneware baking pan that has been buttered and lined with bread crumbs. Bake until done, about 45 minutes.

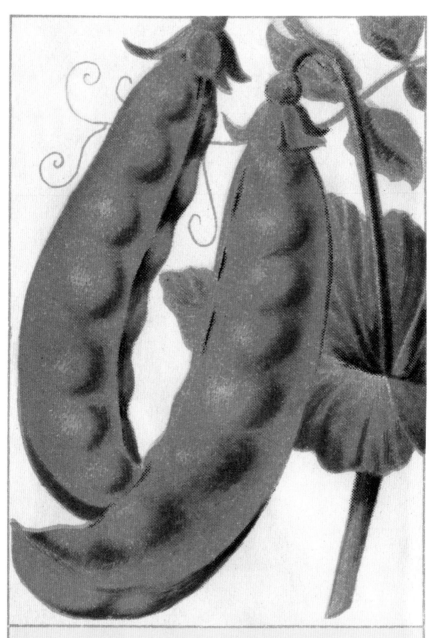

גרינע ארבעסלעך

Green peas

Latkes

CARROT LATKES

Grate 2 large carrots. Add 2 eggs, 2 tablespoons melted butter, a little flour, and some salt. Mix everything well, shape into latkes, and fry in butter like potato latkes until brown.

POTATO LATKES

Coarsely grate 6 large potatoes. Add 1 teaspoon baking powder, 3 egg yolks, some salt, and 2 tablespoons flour, and mix well. Beat the 3 whites into a meringue, and gently fold into the mixture. Shape it into thin latkes. [Fry in butter until brown.] Serve the latkes with sour cream or cranberry sauce.

COOKED POTATO LATKES

Mash 6 pounds cooked potatoes. Add 3 egg yolks, 2 tablespoons flour, and some salt, and mix well. Beat the 3 whites into a meringue, gently fold into the mixture. Shape into latkes, and fry them in butter until brown. Serve the latkes with fruit sauce or sour cream.

RICE LATKES

Following package directions, cook ¾ cup rice [in 1½ cups water] until soft. Add 3 eggs, ½ tablespoon flour, and ½ cup milk. Mix well, and shape into latkes. Dip them in bread crumbs, and fry in butter until brown. Serve with raspberry or cherry sauce.

UKRAINIAN CHEESE LATKES *(SIRNIKES)*

Sieve ½ pound farmer cheese. Mix ¼ cup milk with 1 tablespoon seltzer, and add ¾ cup flour, 3 eggs, 4 tablespoons melted butter, and some salt. Mix everything well with the sieved cheese. Shape it into latkes, and fry them in butter. Now put them in a [baking] pan, and pour on some cream. Bake 20 minutes. You can also sprinkle them with sugar.

POLISH *PAMPUSHKES* (*LENIWE PIEROGI* OR CHEESE DUMPLINGS)

Beat 4 egg yolks with 3 tablespoons melted butter until pale. Mix in 1 pound sieved farmer cheese, 2 cups flour, and some salt. Beat the 4 whites into a meringue, and gently fold into the mixture. Roll out the dough, and cut into 4-cornered [diamond-shaped] pieces. Cook a few at a time in boiling water for 5 minutes. Dress the *pampushkes* with a mixture of 2 tablespoons bread crumbs and ½ cup melted butter.

FARINA LATKES

Cook 1 cup farina in 2 cups milk. Add 3 tablespoons [melted] butter, some salt, and sugar, and beat well for ten minutes. Then add 4 eggs, and mix well. Form the dough into latkes, dredge in flour, and fry in butter until brown.

BUTTERMILK LATKES

Whisk 1½ cups buttermilk. Add salt, 1 teaspoon baking powder, 1½ cups flour, and 3 egg yolks, and mix well. Beat the 3 egg whites into a meringue, and gently fold them into the mixture. Shape into latkes, spoon them into a pan, and fry in butter until brown. Serve with sugar and sour cream.

APPLE LATKES

Peel [and core] 1 pound apples, and cut into thin rounds. Sprinkle with sugar, and leave to rest, covered, for 5 minutes. Meanwhile, beat 2 eggs with ½ cup milk, add enough flour to make a batter for the latkes, and beat well. Melt butter in a frying pan. Dip each apple slice separately into the batter, and fry until brown. Serve sprinkled with sugar.

BLUEBERRY DUMPLINGS

Roll out a sheet of pasta dough, and cut out circles with a glass. Meanwhile, mix 2 to 3 cups blueberries with sugar. Fill the dough circles with the blueberries to make dumplings and pinch to close. Drop into boiling water, add some salt, and cook 5 minutes. Serve sprinkled with sugar and a few tablespoons of sour cream.

[See Potato Kreplekh, page 131, to make pasta dough.—Ed.]

פּעטרעשקע
Parsley

Passover Foods

PASSOVER OMELET

Beat 3 egg whites into a meringue, and gently fold in the yolks. Add 1 tablespoon ground almonds, 1 pinch salt and sugar, 2 tablespoons wine, and 1 tablespoon matzo meal, and mix gently. Melt ¼ cup butter in a pan, and pour in the batter. Cook on both sides over a low flame until brown. Serve sprinkled with powdered [confectioners'] sugar, and eat while hot.

[Use a sweet wine for this omelet.—Ed.]

PASSOVER APPETIZER WITH VEGETABLES AND CHEESE

Thinly slice 3 onions and 2 leeks, and sauté in ¼ cup butter. Add 2 cooked beets, some parsley, and 6 ounces white cheese, and purée everything in a food mill or food processor. Blend the yolks of 4 hard-boiled eggs with ½ cup [melted] butter, and add to the mixture. Add ½ cup matzo meal, 3 raw eggs, and some salt, and mix. Put into a stoneware pot, and bake ½ hour. Then unmold onto a plate, sprinkle with the diced egg whites and some [chopped fresh] dill, and pour on some horseradish sauce.

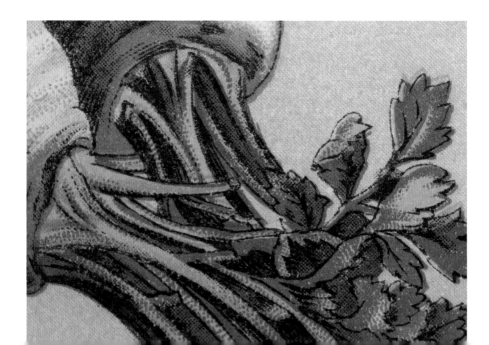

PASSOVER WINE SOUP

Beat 5 egg yolks with 3 tablespoons sugar, and add the zest of 1 lemon. Bring 2 cups sweet red wine and 1 cup water to a simmer, and add 1 tablespoon potato starch dissolved in a little cold water. Gradually beat the wine soup into the yolks, whisking constantly. Then place over a low flame, and continue stirring. When it is about to return to the boil, remove from the heat immediately, and set aside. Beat the 5 whites into a meringue, and add a little sugar. By the spoonful, gently drop the meringue into the hot soup to make dumplings.

MILKHIK PASSOVER MATZO BALLS

Beat 5 egg whites into a meringue, and gently fold in the 5 yolks. Add 2 cups matzo meal, 1¼ cups (2½ sticks) melted butter, some salt, and ½ cup hot water. Mix well, and shape into matzo balls. You can cook these in Beet Soup [see page 38], Prune Soup [see page 31], or milk.

[Refrigerate the batter overnight before forming the matzo balls.—Ed.]

PASSOVER CHEESECAKE

Press 1½ cups farmer cheese through a sieve. Add 3 eggs, ⅓ cup sugar, ½ cup melted butter, 1 tablespoon sour cream, and a little cinnamon, and stir until creamy. Beat 3 egg whites into a meringue, and gently fold in 3 yolks, some salt, and 1 tablespoon sugar. Add to cheese mixture. Meanwhile, soak 4 matzos in water for 5 minutes. Grease a cake pan with butter, and sprinkle with matzo meal. Line with half of the matzos. Pour in the cheese batter, add ½ cup melted butter, and top with the remaining matzos. Bake 25 minutes.

MATZO BREI

Scald 2 matzos in hot water. Mix with 3 eggs and some salt. Then melt ½ cup butter [or less] in a pan, add the matzos, and cook on both sides until brown. This goes with various soups, and also with tea.

PASSOVER TORTE

Beat 12 egg yolks with 2 cups sugar until mixture is pale. Add 1 envelope vanilla powder [or 1 teaspoon vanilla extract], the juice of 2 lemons (not bitter ones), 1 cup cake meal, and ½ cup potato starch, and mix well. Beat the egg whites into a meringue, and gently fold into the batter. Then pour into a cake pan that has been greased with butter and sprinkled with matzo meal, and bake in a not-too-hot oven 1 hour. Allow to cool, slice into layers, and fill with chocolate cream.

PASSOVER NOODLES

Beat 3 eggs with 1 teaspoon potato starch and some salt. Place a frying pan over a flame, and grease with butter or another type of oil. Fry the batter into blintz crepes. Then cut these into thin noodles. They can be used in any soup.

קאפער
Fennel

Substantial Puddings

[Fania's title for this chapter is "Teygekhtsn," which is a type of pudding. An earlier chapter is titled "Pudingen," and of course the kugels are a third type of pudding. The puddings in this chapter are somewhat more substantial and doughy than the lighter pudingen.—Ed.]

BUCKWHEAT PUDDING

(Lithuanians call this *riestainis* and Poles call it *prażucha*.) Brown 1½ cups buckwheat flour with ½ cup fine semolina in a pan. Pour into a bowl, and add salt, 1 tablespoon sugar, and some cinnamon. Pour on enough hot water to make a soft batter. Sauté 1 grated onion in 1 cup [melted] butter, and mix into the batter. Grease a pan with [vegetable] oil, sprinkle with bread crumbs, pour in the batter, and bake in a hot oven 1 hour.

> *[A traditional Polish* prażucha *would also have bacon and salt pork, and would be eaten with milk for breakfast.—Ed.]*

POTATO PUDDING

Grate 2 pounds potatoes, and add 3 eggs, some salt, ½ teaspoon baking soda, 2 tablespoons semolina, and 3 tablespoons white flour. Beat everything together well. Sauté 2 large grated onions in ¾ cup [vegetable] oil until brown, and mix into the batter. Grease a pan with oil, sprinkle with bread crumbs, pour in the batter, and bake in a hot oven 1 hour.

POTATO AND MUSHROOM PUDDING

Soak 2 ounces dried mushrooms until soft, and purée in a food mill or food processor with 2 onions that have been sautéed in butter and 2 pounds cooked potatoes. Then add ¾ cup butter, 6 egg yolks, and some salt, and mix well. Beat the whites into a meringue, and gently fold into the batter. Then grease a pan with butter, sprinkle with bread crumbs, and pour in the batter. Bake 1 hour. Serve with Mushroom Sauce [see page 127].

NOODLE PUDDING WITH MILK

Make thin noodles with 2 eggs, and cook in 1 quart milk until it becomes a thick porridge. Allow to cool. Meanwhile, sieve 1 pound farmer cheese, add ¾ cup raisins, 1 envelope vanilla powder [or 1 teaspoon vanilla extract], 3 tablespoons ground almonds, a little candied orange peel (finely diced), and ⅔ cup sugar, and mix everything well with the cooled porridge. Add ¾ cup melted butter and 4 egg yolks, and mix well. Beat the whites into a meringue, and gently fold into the batter. Then grease a pan with butter, sprinkle with bread crumbs, and pour in the batter. Bake 1 hour.

[See Potato Kreplekh, page 131, to make the noodle dough.—Ed.]

RICE PUDDING

Cook 1¼ cups rice in 2½ cups milk until the rice is soft and all the milk is absorbed, stirring so it does not burn. Allow to cool. Add ¾ cup raisins, ½ cup [melted] butter, 1 envelope vanilla powder [or 1 teaspoon vanilla extract], ½ cup sugar, and 5 egg yolks, and mix well. Beat the whites into a meringue, and gently fold into the batter. Then grease a pan with butter, sprinkle with bread crumbs, and pour in the batter. Bake 1 hour.

FRUIT PUDDING

First, prepare 15 blintz crepes [see Cheese Blintzes, page 76]. Melt ½ cup butter in a pan, and add ¾ cup raisins, ¾ cup diced dried apples, 3 tablespoons ground almonds, ¼ teaspoon almond extract, ½ cup diced candied orange peel, and ½ cup bread crumbs. Mix well, and gently sauté. Then add ⅔ cup sugar and continue stirring until sugar is dissoved. Grease a stoneware pan with butter, and sprinkle with bread crumbs. Lay a blintz crepe in the pan, and spread with the marmalade. Top with a second crepe, and spread with more marmalade. Continue, alternating fillings, until all the blintzes are used. Cover tightly, and bake ½ hour.

APPLE NOODLE PUDDING

Following package directions, cook 6 ounces thin noodles. Add 1 pound diced apples, ½ cup [melted] butter, 1 cup sugar, 1 envelope vanilla powder [or 1 teaspoon vanilla extract], and 4 eggs, and mix well. Grease a stoneware pan with butter, sprinkle thickly with bread crumbs, and pour in the batter. Bake 1 hour.

BAKED BUCKWHEAT KASHA WITH CHEESE

Following package directions, cook 1 cup buckwheat kasha in boiling salted water. Add 1 pound of sieved farmer cheese, ½ cup [melted] butter, ½ cup sour cream, and some salt, and mix well. Grease a stoneware pan with butter, sprinkle with bread crumbs, and pour in the batter. Bake ½ hour.

FRENCH TOAST

Cut a challah into thin slices, dip in milk mixed with eggs, and fry in butter until brown. Serve sprinkled with sugar or drizzled with [maple] syrup.

> [Fania calls this recipe "Fried Gezhankes," but no translation of gezhankes has been found. It sounds like French Toast.—Ed.]

טערקישער פעפער

Red pepper

Sauces and Creams

MILK CREAM

Beat 5 egg yolks with ½ cup sugar. Whisk in 2 cups warm milk. Set over a low flame, stirring constantly, until it is just about to boil. Then remove from the heat, add 1 teaspoon unflavored gelatin [or 2 tablespoons agar], stir, and allow to cool. Beat the whites into a meringue, add 1 envelope vanilla powder [or 1 teaspoon vanilla extract], and gently fold into the cooled cream. This cream is used for charlottes, various babkas, and fruit compotes.

ALMOND SAUCE

Mix 3 tablespoons ground almonds and ¼ teaspoon almond extract with 1 cup hot milk. Add ¼ cup raisins, and cook [gently, without boiling], covered, for 10 minutes. Meanwhile, beat 2 egg yolks with 2 tablespoons sugar, and stir into the almond mixture, whisking constantly, until it is about to boil.

LEMON SAUCE

In a bowl, combine 1 tablespoon melted butter, 1 tablespoon flour, 4 egg yolks, the grated zest of 1 lemon, the juice of 2 lemons, and 4 tablespoons sugar. Mix everything well with ½ cup wine or the syrup from preserves.

APPLESAUCE

Grate or purée 1 pound tart apples. Add ½ cup syrup from preserves and 3 tablespoons sugar, and bring to a simmer. Stir in 1 tablespoon potato starch dissolved in some cold water, and continue cooking for 20 minutes. Then add 4 tablespoons heavy cream. This sauce goes well with various baked goods.

TOMATO SAUCE

Put 1 pound puréed tomatoes in a pot, and add some salt and sugar. Sauté (but do not allow to brown) 1 grated onion in ¼ cup [melted] butter with

1 tablespoon flour. Add the tomatoes, and cook about 20 minutes. Add ½ cup sour cream, and cook about 5 minutes longer.

PRUNE SAUCE

Cook 1 cup [pitted] prunes in 1 cup water [until prunes are soft], and press through a sieve or purée in a food processor. Then add the grated zest of ½ lemon, 4 tablespoons sugar, and 1 tablespoon flour cooked in ¼ cup [melted] butter. Mix well, and bring to a simmer. Add 4 tablespoons cream, and cook about 5 minutes longer.

CREAM SAUCE

In a bowl, whisk together 5 egg yolks, 4 tablespoons sugar, and 1 envelope vanilla powder [or 1 teaspoon vanilla extract]. Bring 1 cup milk to the boil, and gradually pour it into the yolks, whisking constantly. Set over heat, and cook, whisking constantly, until it is just about to boil. Immediately remove from the heat and strain. Stir until cool.

[This is a classic crème anglaise.—Ed.]

MUSHROOM SAUCE

Cook 2 ounces dried mushrooms until soft, 1 parsley root [a parsnip may be substituted], and 1 celery root in ¼ quart [1 cup] water until half the water is gone. Take out the cooked vegetables and mushrooms. Sauté 2 grated onions in ¼ cup [melted] butter until golden, and add 1 tablespoon flour. Continue cooking until brown but not burned. Pour in 1 cup cold water, whisking constantly so that no lumps form. Cut up the mushrooms and some parsley, mix with the sautéed onions, add some salt and ½ cup sour cream, and pour in the remaining mushroom stock. Bring to the simmer, stirring constantly so it does not burn. This sauce is used for various potato dishes [among others].

געלערעפקע
Cole-rape

Stuffed Foods

SEMOLINA DUMPLINGS

In a pan, combine 1 cup milk, ⅓ cup semolina, 2 tablespoons butter, and some salt. Cook, stirring, until thick, and then beat until smooth. Add 3 eggs, and mix well. Drop the batter by the spoonful into simmering soup (Preserved Sorrel Soup, French Soup, Mushroom Soup, and so on). After cooking from 3 to 5 minutes, the balls are done.

TOMATOES STUFFED WITH RICE

Following package directions, cook 1 cup rice in 2 cups salted water. Purée together 2 sliced onions, 1 bowlful sautéed mushrooms (porcini), a little parsley, and some salt. Mix this with the rice, and cook in ½ cup butter. Stir in 2 raw eggs. Hollow out good firm tomatoes, and fill with the mixture. Place in a baking dish, dot with butter, and bake 20 minutes. Make sauce from the tomato insides, and pour over the stuffed tomatoes.

> [Use about 2 cups mushrooms. This recipe will fill about 8 medium tomatoes.—Ed.]

RICE STUFFED WITH MUSHROOMS

Following package directions, cook 2 cups rice in 4 cups boiling salted water until soft. Beat in 4 eggs, and add ½ cup bread crumbs, ½ cup [melted] butter, and some salt and pepper, and mix to form a dough. Soak 2 ounces dried mushrooms until soft. Add 2 hard-boiled eggs, 2 onions sautéed in butter, some [chopped fresh] dill and parsley, and salt and pepper, and purée everything in a food mill or food processor. Make the rice dough into balls, fill them with mushroom filling, roll in bread crumbs, and fry in butter until just brown. Place them in a baking dish, drizzle with ¼ cup [melted] butter, and bake ½ hour. Serve with Mushroom Sauce [see page 127].

CABBAGE *KREPLEKH*

Shred 1 head cabbage, and cook in salted water until soft. Then drain, and sauté in butter with 4 grated onions for 10 minutes. Meanwhile, roll out a sheet of pasta dough. Cut into squares, fill with cabbage, [fold and pinch] into dumplings, and cook in salted water for 5 minutes. Drain, and serve with bread crumbs cooked in ¾ cup [melted] butter.

[See Potato Kreplekh, *below, to make the pasta dough.—Ed.]*

FRIED STUFFED EGGS

Take 4 hard-boiled eggs and halve them, in their shells, lengthwise. Take out the insides [and chop them], leaving the shell halves intact. Dice into small pieces 1 Spanish onion, and sauté in 2 tablespoons [melted] butter. Then soak 1 ounce dried mushrooms until soft, and add 2 tablespoons bread crumbs. Combine everything, including chopped eggs, and purée in a food mill or food processor, adding salt to taste. Add 1 raw egg to the mixture, and fill the eggshells. Dip in bread crumbs, and cook in butter until brown.

[Dip the open side of the egg half in crumbs, and cook facedown in butter.—Ed.]

POTATO *KREPLEKH*

Mix 2 cups flour with 2 eggs and 1 tablespoon sour cream to make a light dough. Roll out the dough and cut into squares. Purée 6 cooked potatoes with 2 onions sautéed in butter and 1 ounce dried mushrooms soaked until soft. Mix in 2 eggs, some salt, and ¼ cup [melted] butter. Fill the squares [fold and pinch to close], and cook in salted water for 5 minutes. Then drain, dress with butter, and bake 15 minutes. You can use these in various soups.

APPLE *KREPLEKH*

Roll out pasta dough, and cut into squares. Grate 2 apples, and add ¾ cup diced large raisins, ¼ cup ground almonds, 6 ground bitter almonds, the grated zest of 1 lemon, some cinnamon, 3 tablespoons sugar, 4 tablespoons bread crumbs, and ¼ cup butter. Mix well, fill the dough squares, [and fold and pinch] to make *kreplekh*. Cook the *kreplekh* in 3 quarts boiling salted water for 8 minutes. Drain, and dress with melted butter mixed with bread crumbs.

[See Potato Kreplekh, page 131, to make the pasta dough.—Ed.]

EGGS STUFFED WITH MARINATED MUSHROOMS

Peel 4 hard-boiled eggs, and cut them in half lengthwise. Take out the yolks, and mash with ¼ cup [melted] butter. Add 15 diced Marinated Mushrooms [see page 181], 1 diced sour pickle, 2 tablespoons cooked green peas, some salt, and mix. Fill the whites with the mixture, and serve with Tomato Sauce [see page 126].

GREEN PEPPERS STUFFED WITH CARROTS

Hollow out 10 sweet green peppers, cook them about 5 minutes in boiling salted water, and drain in a colander. Grate 4 carrots, 3 parsley roots [parsnips may be substituted], 3 small celery roots, and 2 onions. Add some salt and [chopped fresh] dill, and cook in the best oil. Fill the peppers with the mixture. Purée 2 pounds tomatoes, add 1 tablespoon sugar, some salt, and ½ cup [olive] oil, and pour into a large pot. Add the stuffed peppers, and cook 20 minutes. Eat cold.

GREEN PEPPERS STUFFED WITH RICE

Hollow out 10 sweet green peppers, cook them about 5 minutes in boiling salted water, and drain in a colander. Take 3 cups cooked rice, 2 grated onions sautéed in ½ cup [olive] oil, some salt, [chopped fresh] dill and parsley, and

3 eggs, mix well, and fill the peppers. Purée 2 pounds tomatoes, add 1 table-spoon sugar, some salt, and ½ cup [olive] oil, and pour into a large pot. Add the stuffed peppers and cook 20 minutes. Eat cold.

FRIED GREEN PEPPERS

Sauté 10 sweet green peppers in [olive] oil, and peel off their outer skin. Place each pepper on a flat plate, and top with onion, peeled lemon, and tomato that have been thinly sliced. Sprinkle with [chopped fresh] dill, surround with lettuce, and dress with the best oil.

EGGPLANT STUFFED WITH RICE

Hollow out 2 eggplants, and mix the insides with 2 chopped onions sautéed in oil, [chopped fresh] parsley, 4 chopped hard-boiled eggs, [chopped fresh] dill, and some salt and pepper. Add 1 cup cooked rice, 1 raw egg, and 1 table-spoon oil. Stuff the eggplants with the mixture, lay them in a pan, drizzle with oil, and bake ½ hour. Serve with Tomato Sauce [see page 126].

STUFFED KOHLRABI

Peel 4 kohlrabies, cook until soft, and then [halve them and] hollow them out. Meanwhile, dice 2 Spanish onions, and sauté in butter. Add 1 ounce dried mushrooms soaked until soft and some salt, and purée in a food mill or food processor. Mix with 2 tablespoons bread crumbs, ¼ cup [melted] but-ter, and 2 raw eggs. Stuff the kohlrabies. Put the stuffed kohlrabies in a pan with ¼ cup melted butter, cover tightly, and bake ½ hour. Pour on ½ cup sour cream, and bake 20 minutes more.

POTATO DUMPLINGS STUFFED WITH PRUNES

Mash 10 cooked potatoes, add 2 cups flour, 1 egg, and ½ cup water, and knead into a dough. Roll out the dough, and cut into circles. Stuff each circle with a prune (without the pit). Cook in boiling salted water 5 minutes. Then drain, and dress with ½ cup [melted] butter mixed with fried bread crumbs.

TOMATOES STUFFED WITH MARINATED MUSHROOMS

Mix 1½ cups Marinated Mushrooms [see page 181] with ½ cup cooked green peas, 2 hard-boiled eggs, some salt, and 1 diced Spanish onion. Mix everything with ½ cup mayonnaise [see the recipe on page 14], and fill 6 to 8 hollowed-out tomatoes.

RICE DUMPLINGS STUFFED WITH PRUNES

Following package directions, cook 1¼ cups rice in 2½ cups salted water until soft. Add ¼ cup melted butter, 3 eggs, 4 tablespoons bread crumbs, and some salt, and mix. Meanwhile, cook 2 cups prunes until soft and remove the pits. Shape the rice dough into dumplings, and stuff each dumpling with 1 prune. Sauté the dumplings in butter 3 to 5 minutes, place them in a pan, pour ½ cup melted butter over them, sprinkle with sugar, and bake 20 minutes. Then take 1 cup of the leftover prune broth and add ½ cup sour cream and 1 tablespoon flour mixed into ¼ cup [melted] butter. Mix together to make a sauce. When serving, pour the sauce over the dumplings.

קרויט

Cabbage

Baked Goods

MUSHROOM PIES (PIROSHKI)

Make a dough like the one for doughnuts (see the following recipe). Soak 4 ounces dried mushrooms until soft, and purée them with 3 hard-boiled eggs and 4 onions sautéed in butter. Add ½ cup bread crumbs, 6 tablespoons butter, 2 raw eggs, some salt, and [chopped fresh] dill and parsley, and mix well. Fill the pieces of dough, pinch to close, and lay them in a well-buttered pan. Cover, and bake until brown, about 20 minutes. (You may use [vegetable] oil instead of butter.)

DOUGHNUTS

Pour 4 cups white flour into a bowl (the flour must be dry and warm). Dissolve 1 ounce yeast [one ¼-ounce packet dry yeast] in ½ cup milk, and pour into a well in the flour. Knead into a dough. Cover, and leave to rest in a warm place until well risen. Then add 5 egg yolks, 2 eggs, and ½ cup melted butter, and knead into a soft dough (you may also add a little warm milk). Cover again, and set in a warm place to rise. Roll it out, and fill with jam or marmalade. Shape it into doughnuts, and allow to rise again. Melt butter in a pan, and fry the doughnuts until brown, for a few minutes on each side. When they are dry, sprinkle with powdered [confectioners'] sugar.

> [Dry yeast does not dissolve in milk as easily as fresh yeast and needs to be massaged into compliance. Add the eggs and melted butter when the dough is first mixed, or it will be too stiff to knead; also add a pinch of salt and 4 tablespoons sugar. Fry the doughnuts in 2 inches of oil instead of butter, and eat immediately.—Ed.]

FRITTERS (KHRUST)

Mix 2 cups flour, 2 eggs, 1 tablespoon [vegetable] oil, and some salt and 1 tablespoon sugar, and knead into a dough. Roll it out and cut out round pieces with a glass. Cook for a few minutes in butter or oil until brown. Arrange on a plate, and sprinkle with powdered [confectioners'] sugar.

SHORTBREAD CAKE WITH FARMER CHEESE

Knead a dough of 2 cups white flour, ½ cup butter, and ½ cup sugar, and bake in a cake pan for 20 minutes. Beat together 5 tablespoons flour with 3 egg yolks and ½ cup sugar until mixture is pale, and then mix with ½ pound sieved farmer cheese. Beat the 3 egg whites into a meringue, and fold into the cheese mixture. Spread the batter over the baked cake, and bake ½ hour.

[For the shortbread, use only 1½ cups flour. Bake the shortbread in a 9-inch pan at 350°F.—Ed.]

NUT CAKE

Grind 1 pound walnuts with 2 cups sugar, and fold into a meringue beaten from 10 egg whites. Line two 8-inch baking pans with wet parchment paper, and divide the batter between the 2 pans. Bake [about 30 minutes, testing to see if done]. Spread with jam or marmalade. Lay one cake on top of the other, and cover with Chocolate Glaze for Cakes [see page 172].

CHEESECAKE

Measure 10 cups white flour into a bowl. Dissolve 2 ounces yeast [or 2 packets dry yeast] in 1 cup milk, and pour into a well in the flour. Mix into a dough with a spoon. Cover with a cloth, and leave in a warm place to rise. Meanwhile, sieve 2 pounds (4 packages) farmer cheese, add 1 cup sugar, 2 envelopes vanilla powder [or 2 teaspoons vanilla extract], 1 cup [diced] candied orange peel, 1½ cups large raisins, 1 cup [melted] butter, 5 eggs, and ½ cup sour cream, and mix well. Roll the risen dough out into a thin sheet, and lay it on a baking sheet, cutting the remaining dough into thin strips. Spread with the cheese mixture, and lay the thin strips of dough over the cheese in a crisscross pattern. Leave in a warm place to rise; then brush with an egg [wash], and bake until brown.

> *[This dough recipe does not work. Instead, prepare a short dough, such as the one in the recipe for Shortbread Cake with Farmer Cheese on page 139 (double the amount for this cake). The filling is also delicious without the vanilla. Bake in a 10-inch pan at 325°F for 1 hour.—Ed.]*

POPPY SEED CAKE

Cook 4 ounces (1 cup) poppy seeds in water for 1 hour, and drain. Then grind them up, add 8 egg yolks, ½ cup sugar, 1 generous cup sour cream, 10 tablespoons potato starch, and ½ teaspoon almond extract, and beat everything well. Then beat 6 egg whites into a meringue, and gently fold into the batter. Grease a cake pan with butter, sprinkle with bread crumbs, pour in the batter, and bake about 30 minutes.

ENGLISH CAKES

Beat 6 egg yolks with 1 cup sugar and 1 envelope vanilla powder [or 1 teaspoon vanilla extract] until mixture is pale. Add 1 cup plus 2 tablespoons melted butter, 1 cup sour cream, and as much flour as it will absorb. Beat 3 egg whites into a meringue, and fold into the batter. Add 1½ cups thinly sliced candied orange peel, and 1½ cups raisins dredged in a little flour; mix, and scrape into a greased baking pan dusted with bread crumbs. Bake until golden, about 30 minutes.

STUFFED CAKE (CROWN)

Sift 10 cups flour into a bowl. Dissolve 2 packets dry yeast in ½ cup warm milk, and pour into a well in the middle of the flour. Mix into a dough with a spoon. Cover with a cloth, and leave to rise in a warm place. Then add 6 egg yolks, 1½ cups sugar, 4 tablespoons sour cream, and 1 teaspoon vanilla [extract], and knead the dough for 10 minutes (you can also add a little warm milk). Cover, and allow to rise again. Knead again, gradually adding 1 cup plus 2 tablespoons [melted] butter, and allow the dough to rise one more time. Meanwhile, chop 1½ cups candied orange peel, 2 cups raisins, and 1 cup almonds. Mix together with ½ cup bread crumbs, and sauté over low heat in ½ cup [melted] butter. Then mix in 4 tablespoons sugar. Roll out the dough, sprinkle on the raisin filling, and roll it up (making it into a "crown" shape). Lay it on a baking sheet, brush with melted butter, and leave in a warm place to rise. Then brush with 1 egg, sprinkle with sugar and a crumb topping, and bake about 45 minutes. When done, sprinkle with powdered [confectioners'] sugar.

ROLLED CAKE

Mix 1 egg, 3 tablespoons water, and as much flour as will absorb to make a soft dough. Place it on a tablecloth, and roll out until paper-thin; brush the surface with butter. Mix ¾ cup raisins, ¼ cup sliced almonds, a little cinnamon, and ½ cup bread crumbs, and sauté in butter (don't burn it!). Then mix with 2 tablespoons sugar, and spread the resulting filling lengthwise on the edge of the rolled-out pastry. Use the tablecloth to roll up the pastry and filling (using your hands will tear the delicate sheet of pastry). Grease a baking sheet with butter, lay the cake on it, and place in a hot oven to bake, about 30 minutes. When done, lay it on a platter and sprinkle with powdered [confectioners'] sugar.

SHORTBREAD COOKIES FOR TEA

Beat 2 egg yolks, 2 eggs, 1 cup butter, 1 cup powdered [confectioners'] sugar, 1 teaspoon vanilla [extract], and 1 envelope [2 teaspoons] baking powder. Add 4 cups white flour, and knead into a dough. Then roll it out and cut into cookies with a glass. Dip in sugar, place on a greased baking sheet, and bake in a hot oven until golden, about 10 minutes.

STUFFED SHORTCAKE

Beat 6 egg yolks with 1 cup of sugar and 1 teaspoon vanilla [extract]. Add 9 tablespoons [melted] butter, ½ cup sour cream, ½ envelope [1 teaspoon] baking powder, and enough flour to make a soft dough. Roll the dough out into 2 sheets. Spread one with prune butter or jam, and lay the second sheet on top. Lay the cake on a greased baking sheet, and bake until golden, about 45 minutes.

POPPY SEED COOKIES FOR TEA

Beat 5 egg yolks with ⅓ cup sugar until mixture is pale, and add 1 cup of the best [vegetable] oil, ½ cup [2 ounces] poppy seeds, and 1 teaspoon vanilla [extract], and mix well. Beat the 5 egg whites into a meringue, and gently fold into the batter. Add enough flour to make a dough [and roll out the dough]. Cut out cookies with a glass, and dip in sugar. Grease a baking sheet with oil, put the cookies on it, and bake in a hot oven 10 minutes.

CRACKERS FOR VARIOUS SOUPS

Beat 2 eggs. Add 4 tablespoons [vegetable] oil, 1 tablespoon sugar, some salt, ½ cup water, and 4 cups flour, and knead well. Then roll out into little crackers, make holes in them with a fork, and bake on a baking sheet in a hot oven about 5 to 8 minutes.

RYE FLOUR HONEY CAKE

Beat together 2 cups honey, 2 cups sugar (dissolved in a little water), ¼ cup seltzer, 4 eggs, ¾ cup oil, and a few [ground] cloves. Add 4 cups rye flour and 4 cups white flour. Beat well. Put on a greased baking sheet, and bake until done [check after 1 hour]. (Note: You can also fill it with jam.)

CAKE WITH STRAWBERRIES

Beat 1 egg and 3 egg yolks with 4 tablespoons sugar. Add 12 tablespoons melted butter, ¼ cup sour cream, 1 envelope [2 teaspoons] baking powder, and enough flour to make a dough. Grease a cake pan with butter. Divide the dough into 2 parts and roll out into 2 disks that will fit the pan. Place the first half of the dough in the pan, and add 2 pounds strawberries mixed with sugar. Place the second disk on top, brush with egg, and bake until done, about 45 to 50 minutes.

CAKE FILLED WITH CABBAGE

Shred 1 head cabbage (about 2 pounds), sprinkle with salt, and wrap in a cloth to squeeze out the water. Then cook until brown in 1 cup butter or oil. Sauté 1 cup chopped onions separately in 4 tablespoons butter, and mix with the cooked cabbage. Make a yeast dough [see Doughnuts, page 138], and roll it out into 2 sheets. Grease a baking sheet with butter or oil. Lay one sheet of dough on the baking sheet, cover with the cabbage, and cover with the second sheet. Pierce it all over with a fork, allow it to rise, brush with egg [wash], and bake about 45 to 50 minutes.

BUTTER CAKE

Dissolve 2 packets yeast in ½ cup warm milk, pour into 10 cups white flour, and make a dough. Cover, and leave to rise in a warm place. Then add 1 rounded cup sugar, 3 eggs, and ½ cup sour cream. Knead well, and allow to rise a second time. Gradually knead in 1 cup [melted] butter and 1 cup raisins, and allow to rise again. Grease an appropriately sized cake pan, and put the dough in it. Brush with butter, sprinkle with a crumb topping, and bake about 45 minutes. Sprinkle with powdered [confectioners'] sugar.

FRENCH CAKE WITH CHEESE OR APPLES

Make a dough of 2 cups flour, 1 cup [melted] butter, and ½ cup water. Dust the counter with flour, and roll out the dough on it. Then dust dough with flour and dot with some small pieces of butter, fold over the dough, dust the surface with flour, and roll out again. Repeat this 3 times. Fill the dough with cooked apple slices or with farmer cheese, and bake in a hot oven about 50 minutes. When baked, sprinkle with powdered [confectioners'] sugar.

> [This is really just an apple pie if cooked apple filling is used, and is most easily baked in a pie plate. It's unclear why a plain short crust would be filled with plain unseasoned farmer cheese.—Ed.]

OIL COOKIES

Make a dough from 7 cups flour, ¾ cup [vegetable] oil, 3 eggs, 1 cup sugar, ½ teaspoon almond extract, and 2 teaspoons baking powder. Roll it out, and cut out cookies with a glass. Grease a baking sheet, dip the cookies in sugar, lay them on the sheet, and bake in a hot oven about 10 minutes.

EGG COOKIES

Make a soft dough of 5 cups flour, 4 eggs, ½ cup [vegetable] oil, and 3 tablespoons sugar. Roll it out into a thick sheet, and cut into cookies with a glass. Sprinkle a baking sheet with a little flour, put the cookies on it, brush with egg [wash], and bake in a hot oven about 10 to 12 minutes.

APPLE CAKE

Make a soft dough from 4 eggs, 4 tablespoons sugar, 1 cup [melted] butter, 6 tablespoons sour cream, 2 teaspoons baking powder, and as much flour as it will absorb. Divide into 2 parts, and roll out 2 sheets. Place one on a greased baking sheet. Meanwhile, grate 4 pounds apples, mix with 2 cups sugar and 1 envelope vanilla powder [or 1 teaspoon vanilla extract], and spread over the first sheet of pastry. Cover with the second sheet, and pierce with a fork. Brush with egg [wash], and bake about 1 hour.

FILLED CAKE WITH YEAST DOUGH

Make a yeast dough [see Doughnuts, page 138] and divide into 3 parts. Roll out 3 sheets, and lay the first on a greased baking sheet. Thinly slice 2 pounds (4 to 6) apples, and mix with 1 cup sugar and some cinnamon. Spread over the first dough sheet, and cover with the second. Then mix 2 cups raisins, 2 cups diced candied orange peel, ¼ cup sliced almonds, ¼ teaspoon almond extract, ⅓ cup sugar, and ½ cup [melted] butter, and spread over the second dough sheet. Cover with the third sheet of dough, pierce with a fork, and leave in a warm place to rise. Then brush with egg [wash], and bake about 45 minutes.

SPONGE CAKE

Beat 5 egg yolks with 1 egg, 1⅓ cups sugar, and the grated zest of 1 lemon. Mix 5 tablespoons melted butter with ½ cup flour and ½ cup bread crumbs, and blend everything together. Beat the 5 egg whites into a meringue, and gently fold into the batter. Grease a pan with butter, sprinkle with bread crumbs, and pour in the batter. Bake 1 hour. Serve with a Cream Sauce [see page 127].

VITAMIN-RICH FIG CAKES

Cook a syrup of 1 cup sugar and 1 cup water. Meanwhile, chop 10 ounces figs. Add 1 cup chopped nuts, the juice of ½ lemon, and the grated zest of 1 lemon. Add everything to the syrup, and mix well. Then pour it out onto a flat plate, allow to cool, and cut into little cakes.

CABBAGE PIE

Shred 1 head cabbage (about 2 pounds), and sauté with 3 thinly sliced onions in ¾ cup butter until brown. Add 1 teaspoon sugar, and allow to cool. Meanwhile, knead a shortbread dough, and roll out into 2 sheets. Lay one sheet of dough on a greased baking pan, spread with the cabbage, cover with the second sheet, and pinch closed around the edges. Brush with egg yolk, and bake until done, about 45 to 50 minutes.

[Prepare the dough as in recipe for Shortbread Cake with Farmer Cheese, page 139.—Ed.]

CHEESE PASTRY FOR VARIOUS FRUIT SOUPS

Mix together 2 egg yolks, ½ cup sour cream, 2 tablespoons sugar, ½ cup melted butter, 2 teaspoons baking powder, and as much flour as it will absorb. Roll out the dough, and lay it on a greased baking sheet. Sieve 3 packages farmer cheese, add the 2 egg whites, 3 whole eggs, 3 tablespoons sugar, and ½ cup [melted] butter, and mix well. Spread the cheese mixture over the dough, and make a lattice top with strips of leftover dough. Brush with egg [wash], and bake 1 hour.

ALMOND CAKE WITH FILLING

Beat 12 egg yolks with 2 cups sugar until mixture is pale. Add 1 teaspoon vanilla [extract], the juice of 2 lemons, the grated zest of 1 lemon, 1½ cups ground almonds, 1 cup fine bread crumbs, ½ cup potato starch, and 2 tablespoons white flour, and mix everything well. Whip the 12 egg whites into a meringue, and gently fold into the batter. Pour the batter into a greased cake pan sprinkled with crumbs, and bake about 30 minutes. Take out the cake and allow it to cool. Cut into 2 layers, and soak with strong liqueur [such as amaretto]. Meanwhile, cream ¾ cup butter with ½ cup sugar, and gradually add 4 egg yolks, 2 eggs, and ½ cup cocoa [powder], and continue to beat well. Cut in thinly sliced candied orange peel. Spread the filling on top of one layer of the almond cake, and top with the second layer. Pour a Chocolate Glaze for Cakes over the cake [see page 172], and sprinkle with powdered [confectioners'] sugar.

MANDLBROYT

Beat 6 egg yolks with 1⅓ cups sugar. Add 2 cups flour, 1½ cups raisins, and 2 cups chopped blanched almonds, and mix well. Whip the 6 egg whites into a meringue, and gently fold into the batter. Scrape the batter onto a greased baking pan, and bake until golden [about 30 minutes]. Then remove from the oven, allow to cool, cut into slices, and bake a few minutes more.

APPLE CHARLOTTE [SZARLOTKA]

Make a dough of 3 cups white flour, 9 tablespoons butter, and 3 egg yolks. Grease a cake pan, sprinkle with bread crumbs, and press in half the dough. Thinly slice 6 to 8 apples, toss with ¾ cup sugar, and spread over the dough layer. Top with the remaining dough. Bake until done, about 45 minutes.

APPLE BREAD FOR TEA

Prepare a Challah Dough (with yeast) [see page 158], and allow to rise. Meanwhile, peel and core some apples, cook them into a sauce, and pass through a sieve. Knead the risen dough with the applesauce, and allow to rise again. Shape the dough into long strips, lay them on a greased baking sheet, brush with egg, and bake in a hot oven until done, about 45 minutes. Sprinkle with powdered [confectioners'] sugar. (For 8 cups flour, use 2 apples.)

CHALLAH CHARLOTTE

Cut a stale challah into slices. Mix 4 or 5 thinly sliced apples with 1 cup sugar and 1 teaspoon vanilla [extract]. Grease a cake pan with butter, and sprinkle with bread crumbs. Cover the bottom with blintz crepes [see Cheese Blintzes, page 76]. Mix 2 cups cold milk with 3 eggs. Dip a third of the challah slices in the milk-and-egg batter, and lay them in the pan. Dot with 4 tablespoons butter, and add the apples. Then add another layer of milk-soaked challah slices, dot with 2 tablespoons butter, and spread with 1 cup prune butter. Cover with the remaining challah slices, dot with 4 tablespoons butter and 1 teaspoon sugar, and pour on the remaining milk-and-egg batter. Cover with blintz crepes, and bake. Serve with Cream Sauce [see page 127].

SPECIAL BREAD FOR A STOMACHACHE

Pour 19 cups 100 percent whole-wheat flour into an earthenware bowl, and scald with boiling water. Mix well with a spoon, and allow to cool. [Form into dough.] While the dough is still warm, add 2 ounces fresh yeast [or 4 teaspoons dry yeast] dissolved in warm water. Mix again, and leave in a suitable place to rise. Then add another 36 cups of the same flour to the risen dough, as well as salt to taste. Add warm water and knead; set aside to rise again in a warm place 3 to 4 hours. Then form into small loaves, allow to rise, and bake like any other bread.

[This recipe, which calls for 55 cups of flour, has not been tested. Any reader who does so, and can confirm its efficacy in treating a stomachache, is more than welcome to contact us.—Ed.]

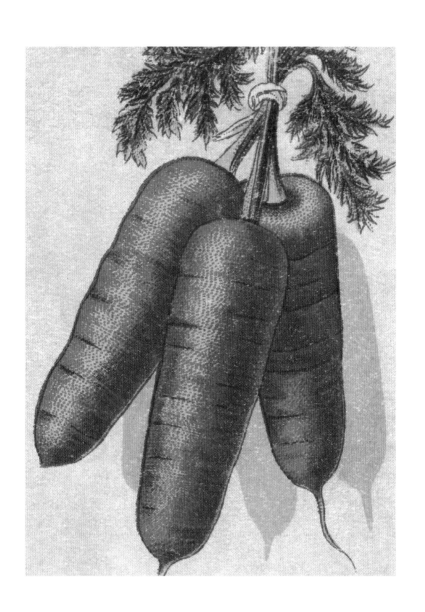

רעטכלעך
Radishes

Jams and Preserves

CANDIED ORANGE PEEL

Soak 1 pound orange peels at room temperature in cold water for 3 days, changing the water 3 times a day. On the fourth day, take out the peels and place in a pot. Cover with boiling water, and soak until the red side becomes soft. Cook 4 cups sugar with ½ cup water, and add the peels. Continue cooking until the peels absorb all the sugar water, mixing constantly to keep it from burning. (Use only the peels of large oranges.)

RADISH PRESERVES

Cook 2 pounds radishes until soft, and cut into long thin batons. Soak them in cold water at room temperature for 3 days, changing the water 6 times. Then drain in a colander. Dissolve 2 cups sugar in 3 cups honey, and add the radishes, 1 cup walnut meat, and 1 cup diced candied orange peel. Cook until brown, and cool with a little cold water.

> [In northeastern Yiddish, preglen eyngemakhts, *literally "frying jam," is the term for cooking the radish in the sugar-and-honey solution. This is traditionally made with a large black radish. If black radishes cannot be found, daikon radish is a good substitute. Peel the black or daikon radish, and cut into 2-inch lengths. Put in cold salted water, and cook about 35 minutes; black radishes will take a little longer. The soaking time may then be shortened to 1 day, with 1 water change (the radishes available to Fania must have been a good deal sharper than those today). After cooking about 30 minutes, some of the radishes become transparent; after 40 minutes, the jam is ready. Finely chop the walnuts, and toast them 10 minutes in the oven. Add them when the jam is almost finished. Cover immediately.—Ed.]*

CRANBERRY PRESERVES

Wash 2 pounds cranberries, and place in a bowl. Cook 2 cups sugar with 2 cups water 5 minutes. Add the cranberries, and cook ½ hour.

[By modern food-preparation standards, Fania's preserves would not be considered appropriately sealed and processed for long-term storage. We suggest storing jarred preserves in a refrigerator or processing them in a bath of boiling water, as per United States Department of Agriculture standards.—Ed.]

SOUR CHERRY PRESERVES

Remove pits from 4 pounds sour cherries. Cook 5 cups sugar with ½ cup water until completely dissolved. Add the cherries, and cook ½ hour. Remove the foam from the surface, and allow to cool. Then add a vanilla bean and pour into jars, wrap in parchment paper, and store in a cool, dry place.

PLUM JAM

Select 4 pounds of the very best, firm, worm-free plums. Pierce each plum with a fork, and lay them in a deep bowl. Mix 3 cups sugar with 1 cup boiling water, and pour over the plums. Allow to rest until cool. Then strain out the juice, cook it again for 3 to 5 minutes, pour it again over the plums, and again allow to cool. Do this 7 times, and then cook [syrup and plums] 30 minutes. When cool, pour into a glass jar, wrap in parchment paper, and store in a cool, dry place. You may remove the pits from the plums and place an almond in each plum.

APRICOT JAM

Pierce 4 pounds fresh, firm apricots with a fork, and lay them in a deep bowl. Mix 3 cups sugar with 1 cup boiling water, and pour over the apricots. Allow to rest until cool. Then strain out the juice, cook again for 8 to 10 minutes, pour again over the apricots, and allow to cool. Do this 7 times, and then cook 20 minutes. When cool, pour into glass jars, wrap in parchment paper, and store in a cool, dry place.

RASPBERRY JAM

In a brass pot for making preserves, place 4 pounds large, fresh raspberries. Pour 1 cup 95-proof spirits [whiskey or bourbon] over them, and add 5 pounds sugar. Leave overnight on ice, in a cool cellar [or in the refrigerator]. Then cook in the same pot ½ hour. Skim the foam, and allow to cool. Then pour into glass jars, wrap with parchment paper, and store in a cool, dry place.

STRAWBERRY JAM

Pick over 4 pounds fresh strawberries, and place in a preserves pot. Pour 1 cup 95-proof spirits [whiskey or bourbon] over them, and add 5 pounds sugar. Leave overnight on ice, in a cool cellar [or in the refrigerator]. Then cook in the same pot ½ hour. Skim the foam, and allow to cool. Then pour into glass jars, wrap with parchment paper, and store in a cool, dry place.

RASPBERRIES WITH CREAM

Rinse 2 pounds raspberries, sprinkle with 1 cup sugar, and pour over them 1 cup cream.

STRAWBERRIES WITH CREAM

Rinse and clean 2 pounds good, fresh strawberries, add 1 cup sugar, and pour over them 1 cup cream.

APPLES WITH HONEY

Peel and grate 3 apples, mix with 3 tablespoons honey, and top with ½ cup whipped cream.

PEARS AND APPLES WITH SUGAR

Peel and grate 2 pears and 3 apples. Sprinkle with 3 tablespoons sugar [or less], and top with ½ cup whipped cream.

APPLE MARMALADE

Peel and slice 20 pounds Antonovka apples (or other tart apples). Discard the seeds, add 10 pounds sugar, cover with water, and cook until thick, mixing so it does not burn. Then pour in an earthenware bowl, wrap with parchment paper, and store in a cool, dry place.

PLUM MARMALADE

Remove the pits from 10 pounds plums. Add 4 pounds sugar and 2 cups candied orange peel, and cook until thick, mixing so it does not burn. Allow to cool. Pour in an earthenware bowl or glass jars, wrap in parchment paper, and store in a cool, dry place.

BLACK CHERRY JAM

Remove the pits from 4 pounds large, fresh cherries, put in a preserves pot, pour on 6 pounds sugar, cover with water, and allow to stand 4 hours. Then cook 30 minutes, skimming the foam, and allow to cool. Pour into glass jars, wrap in parchment paper, and store in a cool, dry place.

ORANGE PRESERVES

Peel 2 pounds oranges, separate into sections, and remove the seeds. Cook 2 pounds sugar with ½ cup water 15 minutes. Add the oranges, and cook 25 minutes. Allow to cool, and pour into glass jars.

איטאליענישע קרויט (וולאסקע)
Italien Cabbage

Turnovers

CHALLAH DOUGH

Sift 8 cups (2 pounds) white flour into a bowl. Dissolve 1½ packages yeast in ½ cup warm water. Make a well in the flour, and pour in the yeast. Stir with a spoon to form a dough. Cover, and leave in a warm place to rise. Then add some salt, 3 tablespoons sugar, 3 eggs, ½ cup [vegetable] oil, and a tablespoon water. Knead the dough well, and leave to rise again. Then [shape into about 4 loaves or braid], allow to rise again, brush with egg, and bake.

[Add the eggs, oil, and additional water when first mixing the dough, or it will be impossible to knead. The first 2 risings will take about 2 hours for the dough to double in volume. For the third rising, preheat oven to 450°F for 1 hour. Lower heat to 375°F when the challahs are put in, and bake about 35 minutes, until loaves are golden brown.—Ed.]

BAKED CHERRY TURNOVERS

Prepare a Challah Dough [preceding recipe]. Wash 2 pounds cherries, remove the pits, mix with 1 cup sugar, fill squares of dough with cherries, [and pinch to seal]. Lay the pies on a baking sheet greased with oil, and leave in a warm place to rise. Then brush with an egg, and bake about 25 minutes.

BAKED APPLE TURNOVERS

Make a Challah Dough [see above]. Thinly slice 2 pounds apples, mix with 1 cup sugar and some cinnamon, fill squares of dough with apples, [and pinch to seal]. Lay the pies on a baking sheet greased with oil, and leave in a warm place to rise. Then brush with an egg, and bake about 25 minutes.

BAKED GOOSEBERRY TURNOVERS

Make a Challah Dough [see opposite]. Wash 2 pounds gooseberries, mix with 1 cup sugar, fill squares of dough with gooseberries, [and pinch to seal]. Lay the pies on a baking sheet greased with oil, and leave in a warm place to rise. Then brush with an egg, and bake about 25 minutes.

BAKED STRAWBERRY TURNOVERS *(PIROSHKI)*

Make a Challah Dough [see opposite]. Wash 2 pounds strawberries, cut them in half, mix with 1 cup sugar, fill squares of dough with strawberries, [and pinch to seal]. Lay the pies on a baking sheet greased with oil, and leave in a warm place to rise. Then brush with an egg, and bake about 25 minutes.

RICE TURNOVERS

Make a Challah Dough [see opposite]. Soak 2 ounces dried mushrooms until soft. Purée in a food mill or food processor with 2 hard-boiled eggs, 1 onion sautéed in butter, and some salt. Following package directions, cook 2 cups rice [in 4 cups water] until soft. Mix the mushrooms with the rice, 2 raw eggs, and 7 tablespoons melted butter. Fill squares of dough with the mixture, [and pinch to seal]. Lay the pies on a baking sheet greased with oil, and leave in a warm place to rise. Brush with an egg, and bake about 25 minutes.

CABBAGE TURNOVERS COOKED IN BUTTER

Make a Challah Dough [see opposite]. Shred 1 head cabbage (about 2 pounds), and massage with coarse salt. Squeeze out excess water, and fry in 1 cup butter until brown; add some salt and 3 diced onions sautéed in butter. Mix well, fill squares of dough with mixture, [and pinch to seal]. Lay the pies on a baking sheet greased with oil, and leave in a warm place to rise. Place in a pan with sizzling butter, cover tightly, and cook a few minutes, until brown. (You may use oil instead of butter.)

POTATO TURNOVERS COOKED IN BUTTER

Make a Challah Dough [see page 158]. Mix 2 pounds cooked and mashed potatoes with 5 tablespoons melted butter, 2 eggs, and some salt. Fill squares of dough with the mixture, [and pinch to seal]. Lay the pies on a baking sheet greased with oil, and allow to rise in a warm place for an hour. Then place in a pan with sizzling butter, cover, and cook until brown. (Oil can be used instead of butter.)

LENTIL TURNOVERS COOKED IN BUTTER

Make a Challah Dough [see page 158]. Pick over, [soak,] and cook 1 cup lentils. Add 3 diced onions sautéed in butter, and purée in a food mill or food processor. Add 5 tablespoons melted butter and some salt, mix well, fill squares of dough with the mixture, [and pinch to seal]. Lay the pies on a baking sheet greased with oil, and leave in a warm place to rise. Then place in a pan with sizzling butter, cover, and cook until brown. (Oil can be used instead of butter.)

CHEESE TURNOVERS (PIROSHKI)

Make a Challah Dough [see page 158]. Sieve 1 pound farmer cheese, and add 3 eggs, ½ cup melted butter, and some salt. Mix well, fill squares of dough with the mixture, [and pinch to seal]. Place in a pan with sizzling butter, cover, and cook until brown.

Make a Challah Dough [see page 158]. Wash 1 pound blueberries, mix with 1 cup sugar, fill squares of dough with the mixture, [and pinch to seal]. Lay the pies on a baking sheet greased with oil, and leave in a warm place to rise. Then brush with an egg, and bake about 25 minutes.

בוריקס
Beet-roots

Compotes and Desserts

LEMON CREAM

In an earthenware bowl, beat 4 egg yolks with ¾ cup sugar and the grated zest of 1 lemon. Squeeze the juice from 3 lemons (without the seeds), pour into the egg mixture, and mix well. Dissolve 1½ tablespoons unflavored gelatin in 3 tablespoons hot water, allow to cool, and add to the mixture. Mix quickly, before it has a chance to set. Then beat the 4 egg whites into a meringue, and gently fold into the mixture. Pour into a mold, and chill. You may serve this garnished with various jams.

APPLE CREAM

Bake 2 pounds Antonovka apples, or other tart apples, and press the pulp through a sieve. Add ¾ cup sugar, and beat until mixture is pale. Then add 1 envelope vanilla powder [or 1 teaspoon vanilla extract], and 3 sheets softened gelatin [or 1 level tablespoon unflavored gelatin dissolved in 3 tablespoons hot water], and mix. Whip 1 cup heavy cream with ½ cup sugar, and fold into the apple mixture. Whip 3 egg whites into a meringue, and gently fold into the apple mixture. Pour into a mold, and chill for a few hours. Serve garnished with jam.

CRANBERRY CREAM

Purée 1 pound cranberries with 2 cups water in a food mill or food processor; squeeze out the juice through a fine sieve or cloth, adding more water as necessary to yield 1 quart juice. Add 1½ cups sugar, and when it dissolves, add 1 cup semolina and cook 10 minutes. Then add 1 teaspoon unflavored gelatin, and cook another 5 minutes. Pour into a bowl, grate into it the zest of 1 lemon, whip until cool, and then add 1 envelope vanilla powder [or 1 teaspoon vanilla extract]. Beat 3 egg whites into a meringue, gently fold into the mixture, pour into a mold, and chill 3 hours.

CHEESE CREAM

Sieve 1 pound of the best farmer cheese, and add 12 tablespoons of the best butter, 4 tablespoons sugar, and 4 egg yolks; beat well. Then add 1 teaspoon vanilla [extract], 1½ cups large raisins, ¾ cup [diced] candied orange peel, and ½ cup heavy cream, and continue beating. Pour into a glass bowl, and garnish with jam.

LEMON CREAM (ANOTHER ONE)

Simmer 2 cups heavy cream with ¾ cup sugar. Beat 4 egg yolks with the grated zest of 1 lemon, and gradually add the hot cream, beating the whole time. Allow to cool. In a glass bowl, combine the juice of 1 lemon with 1 tablespoon unflavored gelatin dissolved in a bit of water, and add to the mixture. Then beat the 4 egg whites into a meringue, gently fold into the cream, and chill 1 hour.

COFFEE ICES

Scald 2 ounces of the best coffee [grounds] in ½ cup boiling water and allow to sit ½ hour. Strain out the grounds and add 2 tablespoons chilled heavy cream and 1 cup room-temperature heavy cream to the resulting extract. Beat ½ cup sugar with 3 egg yolks, and gradually pour in the coffee mixture, stirring constantly so the yolks do not curdle. Pour everything into an appropriate container, add ½ vanilla bean, and chill for a few hours. Serve in champagne glasses, and add 1 spoonful whipped cream to each glass.

GOOSEBERRY DESSERT

Cook 1 pound gooseberries, and press through a sieve. Beat 10 egg yolks with 1½ cups sugar and 1 envelope vanilla powder [or 1 teaspoon vanilla extract] until mixture is pale. Mix ½ cup bread crumbs with the gooseberries and the yolks, and gently fold into a meringue whipped from the 10 egg whites. Grease a baking pan with butter, and dust with bread crumbs. Pour in the gooseberry batter, and bake ½ hour.

ÎLE FLOTTANTE (MILK AND EGG DESSERT)

Beat 6 egg whites into a meringue. Add 1 cup sugar and 1 teaspoon vanilla [extract] to 1 quart milk, and bring to the boil. By the spoonful, gently add the meringue to the simmering milk; when the meringues are ready, after about 2 minutes, take them out and lay them on a plate. Beat the 6 egg yolks. Pour in the remaining milk, beating constantly, and set over a low flame, continuing to beat until it just begins to simmer. Remove immediately from the heat, and pour over the poached pieces of meringue. You may serve with any kind of fruit sauce.

MOCHA KISSEL

Add 4 tablespoons coffee [grounds] to 1 quart milk. Cover, bring to the boil, and set aside to steep 25 minutes. Then strain out the grounds and add 1 teaspoon vanilla [extract] to the liquid, along with 1 cup sugar and 2 tablespoons cocoa [powder], and set over a low flame. Dissolve 2 tablespoons potato starch in 1 cup cold milk, and add to the liquid, stirring constantly until it returns to a simmer. Pour into a pitcher and chill. Serve with whipped cream.

[This is more of a rich drink. For a dessert, double the potato starch.—Ed.]

COCOA KISSEL

Beat 3 tablespoons cocoa [powder] with ½ cup sugar and ½ cup milk. Bring 1 quart milk to the boil, and pour in the cocoa mixture, adding 1 teaspoon vanilla [extract]. Meanwhile, dissolve 1 tablespoon potato starch in a little cold milk, and pour into the cocoa, stirring constantly. Set over a low flame, and continue stirring until it returns to a simmer. Pour into a ceramic bowl and chill. Serve with whipped cream.

[This recipe calls for half as much starch as the previous recipe, which makes it a thinner drink. Adjust starch to taste.—Ed.]

RHUBARB KISSEL

Cook 2 pounds rhubarb in 1 quart water about 20 minutes, and press through a sieve 2 times. Add 2 cups sugar and 1 teaspoon vanilla [extract] to the resulting soup. Dissolve 5 tablespoons potato starch in a little cold water, pour into the soup, and cook about 15 minutes, stirring constantly. Pour into a glass bowl, and chill.

RASPBERRY KISSEL

Cook 2 pounds raspberries in 2 quarts water [about 12 to 15 minutes], and press through a fine sieve. Add 1½ cups sugar and 7 tablespoons potato starch (mixed with a little cold water). Cook about 15 minutes, stirring constantly, and then chill. Serve with whipped cream.

CRANBERRY KISSEL

Purée 1 pound cranberries in a food mill or food processor. Cook in 6 cups water about 12 to 15 minutes, and strain through a fine sieve. Add 1⅔ cups sugar and 6 tablespoons potato starch dissolved in cold water. Cook about 15 minutes, stirring constantly. Pour into a deep dish, and allow to chill.

LEMON KISSEL

Cook 1¼ cups sugar in 4 cups water with the juice of 4 lemons, making sure the lemons are not bitter, about 12 to 15 minutes. Add also the zest of 1 lemon. Dissolve 6 tablespoons potato starch in 1 cup cold water, and pour into the pot, stirring constantly, until it returns to a simmer. Then pour into a pitcher and allow to chill.

LEMON JELLY

Squeeze the juice from 2 lemons. Add 1½ tablespoons gelatin (preferably lemon) [or 2 tablespoons agar], and also the zest of 1 lemon, and combine everything with 2 cups hot water, adding ⅔ cup sugar and ¼ cup sour [lemon] candies, and allow to cook until the gelatin dissolves. Then strain, pour into a mold, and chill 4 or 5 hours, until firm. You may serve this with Cream Sauce [see page 127].

VITAMIN-RICH DRIED FRUIT COMPOTE

Place 1 pound of the very best [pitted] prunes, ½ cup dried apples, and ½ cup dried apricots in a deep bowl. Bring 4 cups water to the boil with ⅔ cup sugar, and pour the hot syrup over the fruit. Then peel 2 lemons (not the bitter kind) and 2 oranges, cut into thin slices, removing the seeds, and add to the compote. You may also add thin slices of candied orange peel. Set aside to chill overnight.

ORANGE COMPOTE WITH WINTER APPLES

Put 4 each thinly sliced oranges and apples in a bowl. Cook 1 cup sugar in ½ cup water with the juice of 1 lemon, and pour the syrup over the oranges and apples. Allow to chill overnight.

WINTER APPLE COMPOTE

Peel 2 pounds apples, remove the seeds, and cut into slices. Lay the slices in a bowl. Cook 1¼ cups sugar in 1½ cups water with the juice of 1 lemon, pour the syrup over the apples, and allow to chill overnight.

RHUBARB COMPOTE

Peel and dice 1 pound rhubarb. Cook 1½ cups sugar with 2 cups water. Add half the diced rhubarb to the syrup, and cook about 12 to 15 minutes. Strain out the rhubarb, and cook the remaining rhubarb in the syrup the same way, making sure it does not overcook. Pour the syrup over all the rhubarb, add ½ vanilla bean, and set aside to chill overnight. You will get the best compote from the thickest, reddest rhubarb.

VITAMIN-RICH ORANGE, BANANA, AND APPLE COMPOTE

Thinly slice 2 oranges, 2 bananas, and 4 tart apples, and lay [them] in a bowl. Separately cook 1¼ cups sugar in 1 cup water with the juice of 2 lemons about 12 to 15 minutes. Pour the syrup over the fruit, and allow to chill overnight.

PEAR COMPOTE

Lay thinly sliced pears in a pan, and add the juice of 1 lemon, 1 cup sugar, and the grated zest of the lemon. Cover tightly, and place in the oven. Stew until the pears become transparent.

BAKED APPLES WITH CREAM

Remove the cores from 6 apples, put 1 teaspoon sugar into each, and bake in the oven until soft, making sure they do not overcook, about 45 minutes. Then cool, and pour on 1 cup cream that has been whipped with 4 tablespoons sugar and 1 envelope vanilla powder [or 1 teaspoon vanilla extract].

VITAMIN-RICH STRAWBERRY COMPOTE

Wash and hull 2 pounds good, firm strawberries, and lay them in a bowl. Cook ¾ cup sugar in 1 cup water with ½ vanilla bean 5 minutes. Then cool, pour over the strawberries, and chill overnight.

VITAMIN-RICH RAW FRUIT COMPOTE

Peel and thinly slice 2 pounds tart apples and 2 pounds pears. Add 2 pounds halved and pitted plums, 1 pound grapes, and 1 thinly sliced lemon. Put everything together in a stoneware pot. In another pot, cook 3¾ cups sugar and the juice of 2 large lemons in 2 cups water, stirring so the sugar dissolves. Pour this syrup over the fruit, and allow to chill 8 hours.

קירבעס
Melon

Glazes and Garnishes for Cakes

SWEET FARFEL [STREUSEL]

Mix together 3 tablespoons flour, 1 tablespoon sugar, and 4 tablespoons cubed butter. Use to sprinkle on baked goods. (You can also make this with oil instead of butter.)

[This recipe is better with butter than with oil.—Ed.]

GLAZE FOR CAKES

Beat ¾ cup sugar with the juice of 1 lemon. Spread onto a baked cake, and return to the oven 10 minutes.

CHOCOLATE GLAZE FOR CAKES

Cook 1 cup sugar in 6 tablespoons milk, stirring so it does not burn. Then add 3 tablespoons cocoa [powder] and 2 tablespoons [melted] butter, cook 5 minutes, and immediately pour over the cake. Sprinkle with powdered [confectioners'] sugar as well.

LIQUEUR FOR CAKES

Peel the zest from 1 lemon, and combine it with 4 tablespoons sugar and 2 tablespoons boiling water. Stir until the sugar dissolves, and allow to sit 2 hours. Then remove the zest and pour in 4 tablespoons 95-proof spirits [whiskey or bourbon], mix, and pour over the cake.

קאפערק

Fennel

Coffee, Buttermilk, and Yogurt

FRUIT TEA (FOR THE SICK)

Slice the peel of 1 apple and some dried apricots, and dry in the oven until brown (do not allow to burn). Add dried raspberries, and brew as a tea.

WHIPPED BUTTERMILK

Pour 4 cups buttermilk into a bowl, and beat with a fork. Then pour into an earthenware pitcher and chill.

COFFEE WITH EGG YOLKS

Brew coffee from 1 cup water and 3 tablespoons good ground coffee. Beat 2 egg yolks with 2 tablespoons sugar until mixture is pale, and pour this into the brewed coffee, beating constantly.

[This recipe is a satiny nondairy alternative to cappuccino.—Ed.]

MATSONI (YOGURT OR "ARMENIAN SOUR MILK")

Mix 1 cup heavy cream with a little warm milk, and pour in 1 quart cooled, scalded milk. Stir, and set aside to sour like buttermilk. It will be ready in 1 day. Then chill.

או ג ע ר ק ע ס

Cucumbers

Marinated Foods

[By modern food-preparation standards, Fania's marinated food would not be considered appropriately sealed and processed for long-term storage. We suggest storing the jarred food in a refrigerator or processing it in a bath of boiling water, as per United States Department of Agriculture standards.—Ed.]

MARINATED RED CABBAGE

Shred 2 heads red cabbage, and blanch twice in boiling salted water. Then drain and place in glass jars. Cook 2 cups vinegar with 1½ cups sugar until sugar is dissolved, and add some allspice and a few bay leaves. Pour into the jars with the cabbage, and store in a cool, dry place.

MARINATED SOUR PICKLES

Thinly slice 30 sour pickles (they should not be too salty). Cook 2 quarts strong vinegar with 3 pounds (6½ cups) sugar, some allspice, and a few bay leaves until sugar is dissolved. Add the sliced pickles, and cook ½ hour. Allow to cool, and pour into jars. Wrap the jars in parchment paper, and store in a cool, dry place.

MARINATED PEARS

Peel and core 6 pounds firm pears, cut each pear lengthwise into quarters, and cook 10 minutes, in just enough water to cover. Then take them out and allow to cool. Cook 6 cups strong vinegar with 4½ cups sugar and 5 cloves, until sugar is dissolved, and pour over the pears. Allow to stand 24 hours. Then cook 20 minutes, and allow to cool. Pour into glass jars, wrap in parchment paper, and store in a cool, dry place.

MARINATED PLUMS

Wash and pit 4 pounds plums, wipe dry, pierce with a fork, and lay them in a bowl. Cook 4 cups mild vinegar with 3¾ cups sugar, 12 cloves, and 1 small piece cinnamon [bark], until sugar is dissolved, and pour over the plums. Set aside [in refrigerator] for 3 days. Pour off the vinegar, bring it to the boil, and pour it again over the plums. Allow to stand for 1 more day. Remove the cloves and the cinnamon, and cook the plums in their brine 10 minutes. When they are cool, pour into jars, wrap in parchment paper, and store in a cool, dry place.

MARINATED MUSHROOMS

Carefully clean [4 pounds] small mushrooms and rinse well in a colander with cold water, until all sand is removed. Place in a pot, sprinkle with salt, and cover with boiling water. Cook 20 minutes, skimming the foam, and then strain. Add some allspice and a few bay leaves and 3 tablespoons vinegar for every 4 cups mushroom broth. Cook a while and allow to cool. Put the mushrooms in glass jars, pour in the cooled brine, wrap in parchment paper, and store in a cool, dry place.

CLARIFIED BUTTER (FOR COOKING, FRYING, AND BAKING)

Buy the best butter in the month of May, and cook it in a large pot until the butter becomes clear, skimming the foam. Remove from heat, allow to stand 2 hours, and then pour the clear butter into an earthenware pot. Refrigerate until it becomes solid. Then cover the surface with a layer of salt, wrap in parchment paper, and store in a cold, dry place. (This is to use in the winter, when butter is very expensive.)

PRESERVED TOMATOES

Peel, seed, and chop about 2 cups tomatoes (or put them through a food mill). Add 1 tablespoon salt and ¼ teaspoon citric acid for every 4 cups. Mix, and pour into bottles up to the neck. Then pour on a little oil, cork, tie up the corks with string so they won't pop out, and store in a cool, dry place.

[The following four recipes are more of historical interest. Before modern refrigeration methods became available to individuals, and when some foods did not have the same year-round availability as they do today, long-term food preservation techniques were an important part of a homemaker's repertoire.—Ed.]

PRESERVED EGGS

Take a clean, sound barrel that does not leak or smell bad, coat the inside with whitewash, and bring to the cellar. Pour 8 buckets water into a second barrel with 16 pounds undiluted whitewash, mix, and allow to stand 24 hours, stirring now and then. Allow to stand a second day, without stirring so the water will separate. Pour the clear, separated water into the barrel waiting in the cellar, and then add eggs, preferably large ones. The eggs can't be cracked, because they would quickly cook in the whitewash. You must check each one to make sure it is sound. When the barrel is full of eggs, cover it so no dirt can get in. The water must cover the eggs.

NOTES:
1. Preserve eggs in the month of May, because then you can be sure they are fresh. Make an effort to buy the large ones.
2. Keep it in the cellar so it won't freeze during the winter.
3. This is prepared for the winter, when eggs are expensive.

SAUERKRAUT

Take a sound, clean, scalded barrel to the cellar. Shred fresh white cabbage, and as you put it in the barrel with a bowl, add to every bowlful of cabbage 1 cup grated carrots, 1 pound sliced Antonovka apples, ½ tablespoon allspice, 1 teaspoon [chopped fresh] dill, 3 tablespoons cranberries, 2 tablespoons salt, and 1 tablespoon sugar. Hammer each layer with a heavy piece of wood, and continue until barrel is full. Take a clean wooden dowel, and poke holes all the way down to the bottom layer of cabbage. Cover the barrel with cloth, and set aside 5 days. Then replace the cloth with clean linen, top with a clean barrel lid, and lay heavy stones on top so it will be well weighted. This needs to stand 10 days. Note: you need to wash the linen and barrel cover every 2 days in cold water so the cabbage stays fresh and does not get moldy.

PICKLED ANTONOVKA APPLES

Take a sound, clean, scalded barrel to the cellar. Cover the bottom with cherry leaves and [fresh] dill, and then fill to the top with layers of tightly packed apples. Put on the lid, and weight it with clean, freshly washed stones. Prepare a syrup. For every bucket of boiling water, add 1 pound sugar, 5 tablespoons salt, and 4 cups molasses. Allow to cool, and pour over the apples until full to the very top. Every day, add more syrup until the apples will absorb no more. In 8 weeks, they will be ready to use as needed.

PICKLED CUCUMBERS

Scald a small, sound, two-sided barrel a few times, and dry it out well. Then cover the bottom with horseradish leaves, celery leaves, cherry leaves, and [fresh] dill. Fill halfway with tightly packed layers of fresh, small, thin, well-washed cucumbers. Then add a small linen bag of garlic and another of mustard seeds, and continue adding layers of cucumbers until full. Cover the top with lots of dill, and also horseradish leaves, celery leaves, and cherry leaves. Hammer the barrel shut, and pour salted water in through the hole (1 pound salt for each bucket of water). Pound the stopper into the hole, and allow to stand 1 or 2 days in the sun. Then store in a cellar, preferably in an ice cellar.

רעטעכלעך

Radishes

Ices

RHUBARB SORBET

Wash and slice 2 pounds rhubarb, cook in 3 cups water until soft, and press through a fine sieve. Add 2½ cups sugar and 1 tablespoon cherry gelatin dissolved in a little hot water, and cook about 10 minutes longer. Strain through a fine sieve, and allow to cool. Then add ½ teaspoon orange extract, pour into an ice-cream churn, and crank until frozen [or freeze in a machine, according to directions].

STRAWBERRY SORBET

Cook 2 pounds strawberries in 2 cups water until soft, and press through a fine sieve. Add 2½ cups sugar, and cook about 10 minutes longer. Allow to cool. Then add 6 egg whites, pour into an ice-cream churn, and crank until frozen [or freeze in a machine, according to directions].

VANILLA ICE CREAM

Beat 2 eggs with 5 egg yolks. Bring 2 cups cream with ¾ cup sugar to a simmer, and pour into the eggs, whisking constantly. Return to the stove and cook, stirring constantly, until it just begins to simmer. Remove from heat, and pour through a fine sieve. Pour into a bowl, and add 1 teaspoon vanilla [extract]. Allow to cool, stirring constantly. Then pour into an ice-cream churn, and crank until frozen [or freeze in a machine, according to directions]. Instead of cream, you can use good, rich milk.

CHOCOLATE ICE CREAM

Cook 2 cups heavy cream with 5 ounces chopped chocolate and ¾ cup sugar [until chocolate melts and sugar dissolves]. Separately beat 2 eggs with 3 egg yolks, and gradually pour the hot chocolate over them, whisking constantly. Return to the stove and cook, stirring constantly, until it returns to a simmer. Pour through a fine sieve into a bowl, add 1 teaspoon vanilla [extract], and continue stirring until cool. Only then pour into an ice-cream churn, and crank until frozen [or freeze in a machine, according to directions]. Instead of cream, you can use good, rich milk.

COFFEE ICE CREAM

Cook 2 cups heavy cream with ½ cup strong [brewed] coffee and 1 scant cup sugar until sugar is dissolved. Meanwhile, beat 2 eggs with 4 egg yolks, and gradually pour this on the hot coffee, whisking constantly. Return to the stove and cook, stirring constantly, until it returns to a simmer. Then pour through a fine sieve into a bowl, add 1 teaspoon vanilla [extract], and stir until cool. Only then pour into an ice-cream churn, and crank until frozen [or freeze in a machine, according to directions].

ORANGE SORBET

Combine 4 cups water, 2 cups sugar, and the juice of 2 lemons and 3 oranges. Cook until sugar is dissolved, and add the zest of 2 of the oranges. Cover, and steep [off heat] 20 minutes. Strain, allow to cool, and add 5 egg whites. Pour into an ice-cream churn, and crank until frozen [or freeze in a machine, according to directions]. Instead of adding egg whites, churning, and freezing, you can serve this as an orange soup, adding a few dollops of sour cream.

RASPBERRY SORBET

Cook 2 pounds raspberries in 3 cups water until soft, and press through a fine sieve. Add 2¼ cups sugar, and cook until it returns to a simmer. Strain again, and allow to cool. Add 6 egg whites. Pour into an ice-cream churn, and crank until frozen [or freeze in a machine, according to directions].

CHERRY SORBET

Cook 2 pounds cherries in 3 cups water until soft. Press through a fine sieve, add 2¼ cups sugar, and cook until it returns to a simmer. Strain again, and allow to cool. Add 5 egg whites. Pour into an ice-cream churn, and crank until frozen [or freeze in a machine, according to directions].

LEMON SORBET

Combine 4 cups water, 2½ cups sugar, the juice of 5 lemons, and the zest of 1 lemon. Cook until sugar is dissolved, and strain. Allow to cool. Add 5 egg whites. Pour into an ice-cream churn, and crank until frozen [or freeze in a machine, according to directions].

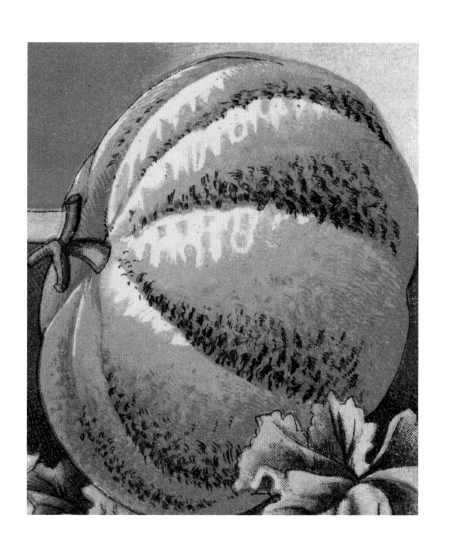

טערקישער פעפער
Red pepper

Wine, Mead, and Liqueur

SPIRIT LIQUEUR

Cook 1 cup sugar in ½ cup water with the zest of 1 lemon and 1 orange until sugar is dissolved. Allow to steep a few hours, then pour into a bottle, add 1 cup 95-proof spirits [whiskey or bourbon], and store in a cool place [or in the refrigerator].

COGNAC WITH EGG YOLKS

Beat 5 egg yolks with 1 cup sugar in a bowl until mixture is pale. Place the bowl over a pan of simmering water [or use a double boiler], and gradually whisk in 1 cup cognac. Keep over heat, whisking constantly, until quite hot and thick. Remove from heat, and continue whisking until cool.

[The following recipes are more of historical interest, recalling a time when many Jewish households made their own wine. Recipes for homemade wine are available today in cookbooks and on many websites. They are not all that different from Fania's.—Ed.]

MEAD

Pour 10 bottles water into a large pot. Use a stick to measure the height of the water, and make a mark on the stick. Add 16 cups of the best bee honey, 2 pounds hard sugar, and 2 cups dark-brown caramelized sugar. Then add ½ tablespoon hops sewn into a muslin pouch. Cook until the liquid is back down to the level marked on the stick. Remove from the burner, and allow to cool. Add brewer's yeast, and allow to rest, covered, in a warm place a few days, until it begins to bubble. Then strain through a woolen bag, pour into bottles, tie muslin around the bottlenecks, and keep in a warm place for a week. Then cork, secure the corks with wire, and store in the cellar. Note: use the mead 6 months later.

STRAWBERRY WINE

Pick over and wash 7 pounds strawberries. Place them in a large glass container with their weight in sugar and 12 cups cooled boiled water. Cover the top tightly with muslin, and set aside 2 months. Then strain through a cloth bag, pour into bottles, cork with good corks, and store in the cellar a few months.

RAISIN WINE

Wash 8 pounds small black raisins, and grind them in a food mill or food processor. Boil 16 cups water in a pot, and then add the raisins. Cover with muslin, and let stand 10 days. Then strain into a second pot, squeezing the pulp well. Add 8 pounds sugar, and mix well. Cover tightly with muslin, and allow to stand 6 weeks. Then strain through a woolen bag, pour into bottles, cork well, and store in the cellar for a few months. (The longer it stands, the better the wine.)

CURRANT WINE

Crush 8 pounds red currants, including the stems, add 16 cups boiled water, and set aside 24 hours. Strain into a pot, squeezing the pulp well. Add 8 pounds sugar, and mix well. Cover tightly with muslin, and allow to stand 3 months. Then strain, pour into bottles, cork well, and store in the cellar a few months.

GRAPE WINE

Combine 16 pounds whole grapes with 5 pounds sugar. Cover tightly with muslin, and let stand 4 months. Then pour the liquid into bottles, strained out of the grapes, cork, and store in the cellar. Cook 6 pounds sugar in 3 quarts water, allow the syrup to cool, and pour over the remaining grapes. Cover, and let stand 4 weeks. Then pour this liquid into bottles, again leaving the grapes, cork, and store in the cellar. Cook 2 quarts water with

4 pounds sugar, allow the syrup to cool, and pour over the same grapes again. Allow to stand 2 months, and then pour into bottles. (The longer it stands, the better the wine.)

ANTONOVKA APPLE WINE

Grate or purée unpeeled Antonovka apples, and squeeze out the juice. For every cup of juice, add 1 cup sugar and ¼ cup water. Mix well, cover tightly with muslin, and allow to stand 2 months. Then strain, pour into wine bottles, cork with new corks, and store in the cellar. (The longer it stands, the stronger the wine gets.)

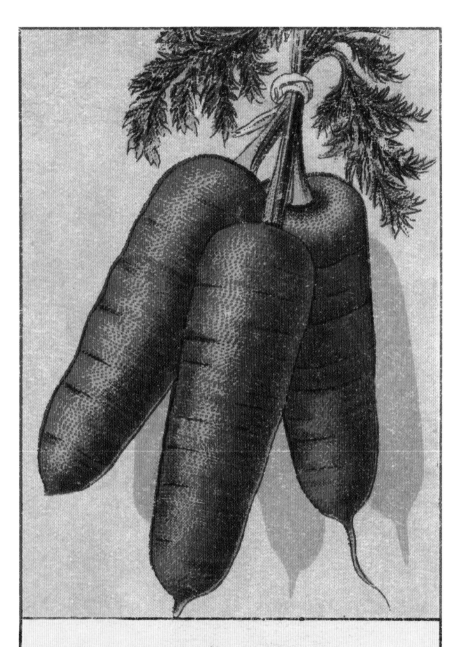

מ ע ר ן

Carrot

Vitamin Drinks and Juices

CRANBERRY LEMONADE

Squeeze 1½ cups cranberries through a sieve and set juice aside. Bring 4 cups water to a boil with 1 cup sugar, allow to cool, and mix with the cranberry juice.

LEMON LEMONADE

Bring 4 cups water to the boil with 5 tablespoons sugar. Allow to cool, and add the juice of 3 lemons.

ORANGE AND LEMON LEMONADE

Bring 4 cups water to the boil with ½ cup sugar, and allow to cool. Then add the juice of 3 oranges and 1 lemon.

ORANGE SYRUP

Bring 4 cups water to the boil with 4 cups sugar and the zest of 1 orange and 1 lemon. Then add the juice of 4 oranges and 1 lemon, and cook 25 minutes. Allow to cool, and pour into bottles.

LEMON SYRUP

Bring 4 cups water to the boil with the zest of 1 lemon and 2½ cups sugar. Add the juice of 5 lemons, cook 25 minutes, and strain. Then cool, and pour into bottles.

VITAMIN-RICH BEET JUICE

Grate 2 pounds raw beets, and squeeze out the juice. Add 5 tablespoons sugar and the juice of 1 lemon. Mix well, and chill.

VITAMIN-RICH CARROT JUICE

Grate 2 pounds carrots, and squeeze out the juice. Add 5 tablespoons sugar and the juice of 1 lemon. Mix well, and chill.

CRANBERRY SYRUP

Purée 2 pounds cranberries in a food mill or food processor, mix with enough water to make 6 cups altogether, and strain through a sieve. Add 6 cups sugar, and cook ½ hour. This syrup is good for tea, babkas, latkes, and so on.

CHERRY SYRUP

Cook 4 pounds cherries in 6 cups water until soft. Rub through a colander and then strain through a sieve until the juice is clear. Pour into a pot, add 4 cups sugar, and cook ½ hour, skimming the foam. When cool, pour into bottles, close tightly, and store in the cellar.

RASPBERRY SYRUP

Cook 4 pounds raspberries in 6 cups water. Then rub through a colander and strain through a fine sieve until the juice is clear. Pour into a pot, add 8 cups sugar, and cook 25 minutes, skimming the foam. When cool, pour into bottles, close tightly, and store in the cellar.

CURRANT JUICE

Remove the stems from 8 pounds red currants, and cook in 8 cups water until soft. Then rub through a colander and strain through a fine sieve until the juice is clear. When cool, pour into bottles, close tightly, and store in the cellar.

Cut up 8 bread rolls (about 2 pounds), and toast until brown. Put the toasted rolls in a large pot, and cover completely with boiling water. Cover pot with a cloth, and allow to stand 1½ hours. Then strain twice through a fine sieve, and add 2 cups sugar. Remove 1 cup warm kvass, mix with 1 packet dry yeast, pour back into the pot, and rest in a warm place 6 hours. Then pour into bottles. Put 5 raisins in each bottle, and rest in a warm place 24 hours. Then cork the bottles, tie up with string, and store in the cellar. On the third day, you can use the kvass. Note: Add yeast only while the kvass is warm (neither cold nor hot). You can use black bread instead of rolls.

EXCERPTS FROM THE GUEST BOOK IN

FANIA LEWANDO'S VEGETARIAN-

DIETETIC RESTAURANT

The vegetarian cookbook by Mrs. Lewando, written in Yiddish, is the first practical guide on how to nourish oneself without meat. The substantial collection of recipes, the thoughtful and well-informed approach to the question, the very successful combinations of vegetables and fruits, and delicious healthy drinks, and the faithfulness to Jewish tradition make this cookbook by Mrs. Lewando a valuable adviser to every homemaker in every house.

—KHANE BLANKSHTEYN

It was a—a—a *mekhaye.*—ITZIK MANGER

> [*Manger is quoting his famous retelling of the Purim story,* Megile-lider. *A* mekhaye *is a life-giving delight.—Ed.]*

The supper was just as Manger said.—Y. GITERMAN

It is written in the Jerusalem Talmud, at the end of Tractate Zeraim: "In the future, one will have to give a reckoning of every pleasant fruit that he saw but did not eat." We praise, therefore, the proprietor of this inn, who does not ruin the cooking and provides pleasure for the multitudes, and say to great acclaim, Go from strength to strength! [In Hebrew.]

—MATISYAHU MIZES

Sour milk according to the Vilne [*sic*] tradition is also delicious.

—LAZAR KAHAN, LEO FINKELSHTEYN, YOSEF DIKSHTEYN

If there were more kitchens like Lewande [*sic*] eating meat would be a *shande* [disgrace].—DR. M. SUDARSKI, *Kovno*

It did not destroy my dear little liver.—YEHOSHUA PERLE

It is delicious, light, and satisfying.—M. BURSHTIN

Perhaps humanity would have a different visage if it were fed without meat.

—SH. VINTER

A message to every Semite and Aryan from one who has been 30 years vegetarian: Gentlemen! Be it known that a lunch at Lewanda [*sic*] is the *milkhik* idea's best propaganda!—A. KACYZNE

To all friends of humanity:
It is no disgrace to cherish animals,
They too grimace
When one gnaws on their stomachs.
They too dream before dawn.
Come, band-of-vegetarians, to the fine, good Lewando!

—M. Y. GROSSMAN

I salute you and your vegetarian dishes.—H. DUBIN, *Buenos Aires*

Your wonderful dishes could turn everyone into a fanatical vegetarian.
—SAM KHIYOR, *Moscow*

Thanks to the friendly proprietor for good, healthy food.—DR. OTTO SCHNEID

They say that the food here is delicious, but unfortunately I came with a delicate stomach and was only able to taste a tiny bit, and it was delicious nevertheless.—MARC CHAGALL, *Riga*

I ate, I enjoyed, and it was light on my stomach.—ZALMEN MAYNZER

My meditations became *pareve* after yesterday's *fleyshik* lunch. It is therefore much easier after a *milkhik* one. It is pleasant.
—Y. BOTOSHANSKI, *Buenos Aires*

Vegetarian food can also be delicious.—G. FAYNERMAN, *New York*

Everyone can be a vegetarian once in a while.
—YUDL MARK, *Kovno and New York*

Not "everyone can be a vegetarian once in a while"! It is everyone's responsibility to be one. You become more human; you are on a higher level when you realize your stomach is not a graveyard, not a "tomb of the unknown" where there are tens or hundreds of living creatures. It is particularly a pleasure and responsibility to be a vegetarian in Vilne [sic], where there is Lewando, the poet of the vegetarian kitchen. Bravo, Lewando! With your obstinate propaganda for vegetarianism, you do more good than those who go on and on about brotherly love.—MARK RAZUMNI, *Riga*

I like this restaurant because it upholds culinary aesthetics.

—NOYEKH PRILUTSKI

Believe me that your vegetarian foods were more delicious to me than many "spiritual foods" from various spiritual cooks.—KHOYSHEKH (DER TUNKELER)

Vegetarianism is much more than simply eating *milkhiks* and *pareve*. Certainly we must eat and eat well. You are therefore due thanks for your successful endeavor in good food. A longtime vegetarian,

—DR. V. OSTROVSKI, *Los Angeles, California*

Your restaurant is not merely a pleasure for the stomach, but also for the spirit. You have already nourished everyone who is anyone. I wish you along with all my vegetarian colleagues the very best.

—D. CHARNEY, *Vilna and Paris*

Although I am not a vegetarian
It is delightful at your place.
When the conversation is delectable
It makes no difference.

—YONAS TURKOV

As an unmerciful beef-, chicken-, and mutton-eater, I can't advertise the social utility of your restaurant so very well. But I can honestly thank you for your welcoming and enchanting relationship to guests and deep responsibility to the calling that distinguishes every superior person at his work. And after this "Hagadah," let me say that your *kneydlekh*—without *gendzen fislekh*—are truly first-class and of the best quality. I wish you all joy and success in the development of your endeavors.—A. MOREVSKI

> *[The Yiddish term for quotation marks,* gendzen fislekh, *literally means "goose feet." Morevski is alluding to the Yiddish expression* "Meynen nit di hagodeh, nor di kneydlekh" *("We don't care for the Hagadah, just the matzo balls"), in which the Hagadah represents all that is spiritual and the* kneydlekh *all that is material. He cleverly uses* gendzen fislekh *in both its literal meaning (no goose feet would be found in Fania's vegetarian restaurant) and its grammatical meaning (he's talking about actual matzo balls and not making a religious statement, and so, he says, no quotation marks are necessary).—Ed.]*

Truly clean, fine, and delicious. If only we could say the same about the rest of Vilna. Do us a favor—come to Warsaw, and we will be frequent guests.

—KH. SH. KAZDAN, SH. MENDELSON, N. BUXBAUM

"You shall eat and be satisfied and say blessings"—we bless the one who feeds and satisfies, and we praise the Lord's messenger who greets everyone with pleasantness and gives merit to those who enjoy his inn. With great blessings,—DR. M. HALEVI, *Bucharest*

> *[Halevi is quoting Deuteronomy 8:10, which also appears in the traditional grace after meals.—Ed.]*

BIOGRAPHICAL SKETCHES FROM THE GUEST BOOK

KHANE BLANKSHTEYN (1861?–1939), a nurse and community activist who learned Yiddish as an adult and was an unsuccessful candidate for the Polish parliament. She wrote essays and short stories for several Vilna newspapers.

YANKEV (IAKOB) BOTOSHANSKI (1892/95–1964) was a journalist, playwright, and community activist. He moved to Argentina in 1926.

MIKHAL BURSHTIN (1897–1945) was a novelist and historian of the First World War.

MARC CHAGALL (1887–1985), possibly one of the world's most important and admired modern artists, is best known as a painter. He illustrated countless Yiddish books and journals, and designed sets and stained-glass windows for the Metropolitan Opera in New York.

DANIEL CHARNEY (1888–1959) was a poet and the editor of the Communist Yiddish paper *Der Emes*. He wrote critically of Soviet spelling reform of the Yiddish language, causing some tension within the Party. He was admitted to the United States in 1941. He was the brother of the critic Shmuel Niger and the social activist Borekh Charney-Vladek.

LEO FINKELSHTEYN (1895–1950), a journalist and community activist published in both Yiddish and Polish.

YITSKHAK GITERMAN (1889–1943) was one of Warsaw's most devoted community activists, and director of the Joint Distribution Committee in Poland.

ALTER KACYZNE (1885–1941) is best known for his evocative photography detailing the everyday lives of Polish Jews. He was also a gifted writer of poetry, prose, and drama.

LAZAR KAHAN (1885–1946) published articles on politics and popular science and attended the Czernowitz Conference of 1908. He survived the war in Japan and Shanghai.

KHAYIM SHLOYME KAZDAN (HAYYIM SOLOMON KAZDAN) (1883–1979), one of the founders of the Central Yiddish School organization, was a political activist particularly associated with the Bund. He arrived in the United States in 1941, where he continued to teach and write about education and activism in Poland.

ITZIK MANGER (1901–1969) is one of the best-known and most beloved Yiddish poets. His *Khumesh Lider (Torah Songs)* and *Megile-lider (Megillah Songs)* offer satiric retellings of familiar stories from the Hebrew Bible.

YUDL MARK (1897–1975), one of the most important and influential scholars of the Yiddish language and linguistics, was author of *Grammar of Standard Yiddish* and editor of *Der Groyser Verterbukh fun der Yiddisher Shprakh.*

SHLOYME MENDELSON (1896–1948) was a literary critic and political activist associated with the Bund and the Folkspartei. He came to the United States in 1941.

MATISYAHU MIZES (MATTHIAS MIESES) (1885–1945), a philologist, was the author of hundreds of political and scholarly articles in Yiddish and Hebrew.

AVROM MOREVSKI (MENAKER) (1886–1964) was an actor in the Russian theater and the Yiddish theater. He was also a director and translator of theatrical pieces. He survived the war in the Soviet Union and returned to Poland in 1956.

YEHOSHUA PERLE (1888–1943) was the author of many acclaimed stories and novels, among them "Yidn fun a Gants Yor" ("Everyday Jews"), a gritty, hyper-realistic portrait of life in Poland.

NOYEKH PRILUTSKI (NOAH PRYŁUCKI) (1882–1941), a pioneer in the study of Yiddish dialects and ethnography, was one of the founders of the YIVO Institute. He was also an ardent community activist and served in the Polish parliament.

MARK RAZUMNI (1896–1988) was a journalist, humorist, translator, and dramaturg. He survived the war in Tashkent.

DR. OTTO SCHNEID (1900–1974) was a painter, sculptor, and art historian who worked with YIVO's collection of Jewish art in Vilna.

DR. MENDL SUDARSKI (1885–1951) wrote about medicine, Yiddish theater, and literature, and Jewish subjects in general. He immigrated to New York in 1937.

YONAS TURKOV (JONAS TURKOW) (1898–1988) was an actor on the Yiddish stage in Poland and a theater director in the Warsaw Ghetto. He settled in Israel in 1966.

SHMUEL VINTER (1891–1943) was a prolific Yiddishist, linguist, and geographer. He successfully lobbied the post office of Włocławek, Poland, to send and receive telegrams in Yiddish. Vinter was among the researchers of Operation Oneg Shabbat in the Warsaw Ghetto.

DER TUNKELER (YOSEF TUNKL) (1881–1949), a caricaturist and humorist, was the founder of *Der Groyser Kundes,* New York's famous satiric periodical.

ACKNOWLEDGMENTS

From the moment in 2009 when we laid eyes on Fania Lewando's beautifully illustrated *Vegetarish-Dietisher Kokhbukh*, written in Yiddish and published in Vilna in 1938, we began thinking about how to find a way to share the book with modern readers. Fania's helpful lessons in nutrition for "housewives" combined with her delicious vegetarian recipes seemed so far ahead of their time, but also felt contemporary to the 1930s. We hope that the publication of her book in English will give this extraordinary woman a voice in the twenty-first century and will give her readers a glimpse into vegetarianism 1930s style and into Jewish life in Vilna between the world wars.

We would like to thank Joan Nathan for her foreword, which provides a culinary context for the book. And we would also like to thank her for connecting us with Altie Karper at Schocken Books, without whom this book would not have been published. Thanks also to Professor Efraim Sicher for his introduction, which provides a historical context for the book and which gives us a wonderful background to the life of his great-aunt Fania. We are grateful to Jonathan Brent, executive director of the YIVO Institute for Jewish Research, for supporting the project from its inception and for sharing his vast knowledge and network of contacts in the publishing world. We would like to thank Eve Jochnowitz for her exhaustive knowledge and expertise in Yiddish-language Jewish cuisine. Her passions for Yiddish literature and specifically for keeping Fania Lewando's memory alive were invaluable. Thanks also to Aviva Astrinsky, former Head Librarian of YIVO, who first shared the original Yiddish-language book with us. She unearthed an absolute gem in YIVO's rare book room. And our thanks to Ruth Levine and Rosina Abramson for providing the initial seed money and for their enthusiastic support.

We would also like to thank Sonia Shannon, who fueled the project with her creativity, artistry, and ability to bring historical imagery to life; Patricia Anders for her attention to detail in copyediting the first draft of the manuscript; Esther Bromberg of the Museum of Jewish Heritage for sharing the publicity brochure Fania created for her cookbook, which provided critical biographical information; DeeDee Lichtenberg Scanlan for designing our first recipe card and mailing; and Dr. Lyudmila Sholokhava, Acting Chief Archivist at YIVO, for helping us navigate through YIVO's archives.

Finally, and most important, Altie Karper and Lexy Bloom at Schocken Books transformed this humble project into a book that gives the world an opportunity to learn about Fania Lewando and this special place and time in Jewish history.

We would like to thank the following individuals for their generous support in getting *The Vilna Vegetarian Cookbook* translated and designed: George Abrahams, Jeffrey E. Glen and Rosina K. Abramson, Aviva E. Astrinsky, Theodossios and Elaine Athanassiades, Virginia Bayer and Robert Hirt, Herman A. Bursky, Lainie Charmatz, Lawrence and Jane Cohen, David and Concetta Dattilo, Mitchell and Jill Friedman, Robert and Fran Geier, Meredith Gantcher, Elissa Hutner, Gary and Diane Katz, Deborah S. Katz-Downie and Stephen R. Downie, David and Ruth Levine, Joseph and Rona Lupkin, Stanley and Laurie Maurer, Edward and Sharon Mazur, Lee and Rebecca Miller, the Nash Family Foundation, Michael and Janet Ramer, Rachel M. Ringler and Seth Siegel, Marcie Rosenberg, Anna Sabat Wolin, Stella Skura, Carol A. L. Stahl, Herman and Myra Treitel, and Mira Jedwabnik van Doren. And finally, special thanks to Charles Dimston, whose initial and significant generosity was instrumental in making this project a reality.

BARBARA MAZUR AND WENDY K. WAXMAN,
on behalf of the YIVO Institute for Jewish Research

INDEX

R

radish:
    Preserves, 152
    Salad, 16
raisin(s):
    Apple Charlotte with Whole-Wheat
        Bread Crumbs, 102–3
    Apple Pudding, 103
    Bread Crumb Kugel, 98
    Challah Kugel, 97–8
    Cheesecake, 139–40
    Cheese Cream, 164–5
    Crepe Kugel with Jam, 97
    English Cakes, 140
    Fruit Pudding, 121
    Mandlbroyt, 147
    Noodle Kugel, 96
    Noodle Pudding with Milk, 121
    Pudding with Blintz Wrappers
        Layered with Cheese, 104
    Rice Kugel, 96–7
    Rice Pudding, 121
    Rice with, 62
    Rolled Cake, 141
    Stuffed Cake (Crown), 140–1
    Toasted Kugel, 98
    Wine, 193
raspberry(ies):
    with Cream, 154
    dried, in Fruit Tea (for the Sick), 176
    Jam, 154
    Kissel, 167
    Mousse, 72
    Sorbet, 187
    Syrup, 199
Raw Fruit Compote, Vitamin-Rich,
    169

rhubarb:
    Blintzes, 76
    Compote, 168
    Kissel, 166–7
    Sorbet, 186
    Soup, 32
rice:
    Apple Pudding with, 103
    with Apples, 62
    Dumplings, 66
    Dumplings Stuffed with Prunes, 134
    Eggplant Stuffed with, 133
    with Eggs, 67
    with Farmer Cheese, 62
    Frittata, 92
    Green Peppers Stuffed with, 132–3
    Kugel, 96–7
    Latkes, 108
    with Mushrooms, 62
    and Mushroom Soup, 30
    Porridge, 86
    Pudding, 121
    with Raisins, 62
    Soup with Milk, 35
    Soup with Water, 34
    Stewed, with Dutch Cheese, 53–4
    Stewed Cabbage with, 51
    with Strawberries, 63
    Stuffed with Mushrooms, 130
    with Swiss Cheese, 63
    Tomatoes Stuffed with, 130
    Turnovers, 159
    with Whipped Cream, 63
Riestainis (Lithuanian Buckwheat
    Pudding), 120
roll(s):
    Apple Pudding, 103